The book, an extraordinary revelation of a complex, perceptive mind, wipes out the shallow popular image of Geronimo as only a crafty, fanatically bloodthirsty fighter.

Geronimo begins his autobiography with an account of the Apache creation story and cosmology, then moves on to tell his own story, from his birth near the headwaters of the Gila River in 1829 to final surrender to army troops in 1886.

His story is by no means wholly one of violent action. He relates out of vivid memory and with wonderful descriptive powers the origins and customs of the Apache people, his relatively happy early life, tells of his family and of his life as a prisoner, of the unwritten laws of the Apaches, his religion, and finally, of his vision of the future for his people.

"An heroic story, eloquently told. It is also a reminder of the conscienceless sweep of American 'manifest destiny' which has left in its wake the continuing plight of the land's aborigines."
—*San Francisco Examiner*

GERONIMO
His Own Story

Edited by
S. M. BARRETT

*Newly edited with
an Introduction and Notes by*
Frederick W. Turner III

BALLANTINE BOOKS • NEW YORK

The map, Apache Country, 1865–1886, is reproduced
with the permission of Charles Scribner's Sons from *The
Atlas of American History,* edited by James Truslow
Adams © 1943

Library of Congress Catalog Card Number: 72-113457

SBN 345-22238-5-125

This edition published by arrangement with
E. P. Dutton & Co., Inc.

First Printing: May, 1971
Second Printing: September, 1971
Third Printing: April, 1972
Fourth Printing: February, 1973
Fifth Printing: April, 1974
Sixth Printing: September, 1974

First Canadian Printing: May, 1971

Cover photograph by A. Frank Randall: Courtesy of
The Arizona Pioneers' Historical Society, Tucson

Printed in the United States of America

BALLANTINE BOOKS
A Division of Random House, Inc.
201 East 50th Street, New York, N.Y. 10022

DEDICATORY

Because he has given me permission to tell my story; because he has read that story and knows I try to speak the truth; because I believe that he is fair-minded and will cause my people to receive justice in the future; and because he is chief of a great people, I dedicate this story of my life to Theodore Roosevelt, President of the United States.

GERONIMO

CONTENTS

ACKNOWLEDGMENTS

The publisher gratefully acknowledges the kindness of Mr. Thomas G. Bazler, Librarian, and the staff of the American Museum of Natural History Library in making available the original text of *Geronimo's own story*. To Mr. Gillett Griswold, Director of the U.S. Army Museum at Fort Sill, Oklahoma, thanks are also due for his help in supplying complete and accurate captions for the photographs in the original text, for the copy of Geronimo's signature and for other aids.

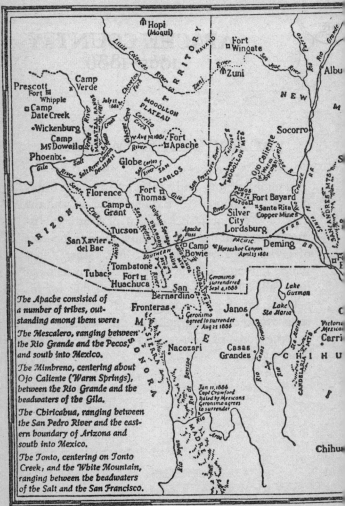

The Apache consisted of a number of tribes, outstanding among them were:

The Mescalero, ranging between the Rio Grande and the Pecos, and south into Mexico.

The Mimbreno, centering about Ojo Caliente (Warm Springs), between the Rio Grande and the beadwaters of the Gila.

The Chiricabua, ranging between the San Pedro River and the eastern boundary of Arizona and south into Mexico.

The Tonto, centering on Tonto Creek, and the White Mountain, ranging between the beadwaters of the Salt and the San Francisco.

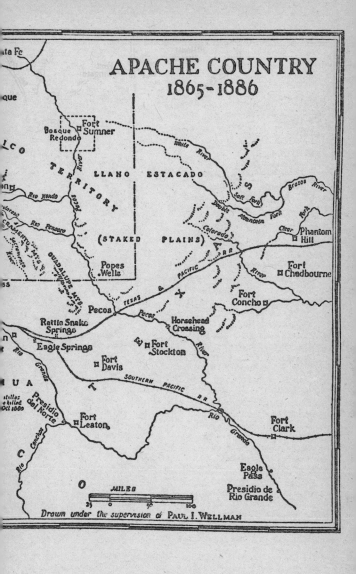

APACHE COUNTRY
1865-1886

Drawn under the supervision of PAUL I. WELLMAN

PREFACE

THE initial idea of the compilation of this work was to give the reading public an authentic record of the private life of the Apache Indians, and to extend to Geronimo as a prisoner of war the courtesy due any captive, *i.e.*, the right to state the causes which impelled him in his opposition to our civilization and laws.

If the Indians' cause has been properly presented, the captives' defense clearly stated, and the general store of information regarding vanishing types increased, I shall be satisfied.

I desire to acknowledge valuable suggestions from Major Charles Taylor, Fort Sill, Oklahoma; Dr. J. M. Greenwood, Kansas City, Missouri; and President David R. Boyd, of the University of Oklahoma.

I especially desire in this connection to say that without the kindly advice and assistance of President Theodore Roosevelt this book could not have been written.

Respectfully,
S. M. BARRETT.

LAWTON, OKLAHOMA.
August 14, 1906.

GERONIMO

INTRODUCTION
By Frederick W. Turner III

In view of this battle one may ask—What separates the enlightened man from the savage? Is civilization a thing distinct, or is it an advanced stage of barbarism?

—HERMAN MELVILLE.

I

ON a warm May morning in 1862 Henry David Thoreau, scion of the fading Eastern literary establishment, lay gasping out his life in his Concord bed. Tender hands raised him once more to a sitting position as he murmured his last words: "Moose . . . Indian . . ."and put life away. What did he mean by that?

The question is captious. We know that since his first trip to Maine almost ten years earlier Thoreau had been interested in Indians and at last had determined to write a book about them.

1

Still, let us hold on to this slight historical moment to ask what it was about Indians that came to fascinate the philosopher/naturalist, for surely by the 1850s little could have been left of the aboriginal vigor once belonging to the Indians of the Northeastern Woodlands. It has been axiomatic in this country that for the Indian civilization corrupts absolutely, and the pitifully few survivors of the Eastern Woodlands' once-populous nations could hardly have escaped the effects of the Bible, the sword, and the jug.

So it must have been something more than the present moment that caught Thoreau's omnivorous eye; it must have been what he sensed had once been true of the Indian that drew his attention and his sympathy. What Thoreau sensed was that the Indian had once stood in reverent proximity to the natural world, that rather than attempting to subdue and subvert it he had offered himself to it in order to live with it, and that in so doing he had, in the wishful words of Robert Frost, "found salvation in surrender." And this attitude was precisely what Thoreau missed among the Indian's conquerors of his own day.

By the middle years of the nineteenth century when Thoreau wrote *Walden*, man's technological progress had allowed him to forget the vital interdependence between himself and the landscape—at least this was so in the subdued environs of the East. The consequences of this loss of reverence, of this grossly inaccurate perspective, were many, and it is fair to say a century after Thoreau's death that he saw most of them clearly.

But the root consequence, the one which gave rise to all the others, was an unwarranted pride, a kind of moral giganticism, the kind of perspective that allows man to see himself as the largest thing on the landscape after he has cut down all the trees. "We need the tonic of wildness," Thoreau wrote in *Walden*,

> to wade sometimes in marshes where the bittern and the meadow-hen lurk, and hear the booming of the snipe; to smell the whispering sedge where only some wilder and more solitary fowl builds her nest, and the mink crawls with its belly close to the ground. At the same time that we are earnest to explore and learn all things, we require that all things be mysterious and unexplorable, that land and sea be infinitely wild, unsurveyed and unfathomed by us because unfathomable. We can never have enough of nature. We must be refreshed by the sight of inexhaustible vigor, vast and titanic features, the sea-coast with its wrecks, the wilderness with its living and its decaying trees, the thunder cloud, and the rain which lasts three weeks and produces freshets. *We need to witness our own limits transgressed, and some life pasturing freely where we never wander.*

The italics of the last sentence are mine, for they represent to me the heart of everything Thoreau had to say about our culture, from *Walden* through to the last essays like "Walking." The prophetic voice which speaks through all his pages is the one that says that Progress which is achieved at the expense of everything else—the

natural world, other cultures, proper perspective
—is bound to be consumed by itself.

By the midpoint of the last century it was possible for Thoreau and others to regard progress
in America in some kind of historical dimension:
the eastern third of the country was already well
settled; the forests had been pruned to groves;
railroads cut close to even the most bucolic
ponds; smokestacks thrust themselves higher than
the tallest tree; and to look westward was to fore-
see the not-too-distant completion of manifest
destiny.

But the crucial difference between Thoreau
and most of his fellow Americans was that he
wondered if the price of Progress was not too
high. And now with our new worlds to conquer
we can and must ask the same question.

We must ask what it is we are destroying in
ourselves and others in this mad lust for adventure
which we choose to call Progress and whether
in the process of Progress we are forgetting—
have already forgotten—what it means to be
men. The exploration and exploitation of space
is but the latest, and perhaps one of the very last,
chapters in the story of Western white man's
ruthless trek toward that absolute supremacy
over the universe that he once assigned to the
gods and that he dares not admit was once theirs.
"Such an abuse of legitimate adventure," write
the editors of a recent collection of essays on
ecology, "has been chronic in the modern western world since the Portuguese and the Spanish
powers strove to meet the challenge of the seas,

the heathens, and the unexploited lands." With one New World conquered, with its aboriginal inhabitants but nagging memories and public nuisances, and with new worlds yet to conquer, we must look as Thoreau did at the meaning of our actions.

Which brings us back to the very beginning of the process when Hernando Cortés landed on the shores of Mexico with five hundred and eight soldiers, sixteen horses, some brass guns, and four falconets. Doubtless Cortés did not ask himself at this point, whether this trip was necessary, for something in the culture of the West had already told him it was. He was but an instrument of history as he stood on those mosquito-infested sands and ordered his men to burn the ships so that there could be no turning back. There could be no turning back, for whatever force it was that sent the Norse out upon the pitiless seas to sail they knew not where, perhaps to fall off the edge of the world into the waiting maws of monsters, and maybe even before them the Phoenicians, had sent Cortés on the trail of his country men to Cuba and from there to Mexico as surely as if he had been a toy soldier held between the thumb and forefinger of a hand moving over a toy terrain. No matter. Cortés gave his men a lecture about the destiny that history had marked out for them, drawing his precedent from Caesar's speech to his legions in Gaul, and marched westward. It was the middle of August 1519.

The specific goals seem to have been gold, territory, and glory in about that order, and all three of these subsumed under the name of Progress. True as these goals may have seemed at the time, the real situation may have been closer to that suggested in a remark which Cortés is reported to have made to an Indian who had the base ignorance to ask what it was that the Spaniards found so attractive about gold. The Spaniards, Cortés replied, suffer from a disease of the heart for which gold is the only remedy.

Cortés's conquest of the Aztecs provides us with a model for all subsequent red/white relations in the New World, for this Western white conquered as much by promises and by exploiting tribal divisions as by force of arms. He was also aided by smallpox—the first communicable disease to infect the new continent—which took among its victims the successor to the murdered Moctezuma who had thought, as other and later Indian leaders were to think, that he could appease the whites with a few presents and expressions of good will.

In destroying the Aztecs and then the Incas, the Spaniards were still on familiar ground despite the strange customs of their adversaries. They were, after all, sieging cities and capturing empires, and this was a game that had been played for a long time in the Old World. But when Cortés's countryman, Francisco Vazquez de Coronado, journeyed into the deserts of the American Southwest, the rules of the game were changed considerably. Here there were no cities of gold, there were no definable empires to claim in the names of king and Christ, and by the time the expedition's major chronicler, Pedro Castañeda de Nájera, casually mentioned running across some nomadic desert folk who would someday be known as Apache, the men were wishing more for water than for riches. This was a very different sort of cultural clash, and to understand it is to understand the anthropological meaning of the long campaign to rid the North American portion of the New World of its original inhabitants.

It was, firstly, a clash between a culture essentially progressive in its self-image and in its aspirations and a group of related cultures that were essentially static, that is, cultures which saw themselves as important and vital but not as moving toward any collective millennium. It was a clash between a culture that had a fear of nature until it could subdue it and a contempt for it once it had been subdued and cultures that thought of themselves as participating with the natural world in the huge cycle of life. It was a clash between a culture that, though at first and of necessity was agriculturally oriented, always cherished a mercantile image of itself and strove mightily to fulfill that image and cultures devoted to simple agriculture and hunting. It was a clash between a culture with an abstract numismatic system and those who dealt always in the concrete and consumable. Finally, and most unfortunately for the losers, it was a clash between a culture that fought for territorial conquest and cultures for which warfare was as much ritual as anything else and for which the idea of permanent territorial acquisition was impractical.

On the face of it then, and leaving aside the relative technological levels, it was a cultural clash that the parties of the second part could not hope to win, as indeed we know they did not. In every crucial respect the Indian was at a disadvantage in his conflict with the whites, and at this remove the conquest of the continent has an iron inevitability about it which has become so familiar to us that we can call it history. But if we persist in thinking of this as the history of how the white man made America, we will continue to miss the great lesson that this culture clash has to teach us, for as Roy Harvey Pearce has pointed out, in America from the very beginning the history of the savage has been the history of the civilized. They are inseparable parts of one chronicle, more so now that we can look back upon it and ask those crucial questions which Thoreau was asking before us. But in order to ask those questions we must do no less than imagine ourselves as Indians, so as to unite the now separate strands of this chronicle and see it as the story of men ruled unwillingly and otherwise by the idea of Progress and marching under that banner toward the setting sun, only to discover when we arrived at the journey's end that we had lost on the way whatever it was we hoped to find: peace? contentment? the good life? And so now, off again on a new journey, hoping to find on a dead planet what we have largely killed on this one.

We marched on the journey together—red and white—for almost four hundred years before it reached its bloody and frozen ending in the snows at Wounded Knee, and the last of the Indian uprisings could be entered as history and thus past. The great fact was now accomplished: Progress had extirpated its last enemies, Frederick Jackson Turner could announce at the ex-Indian village of Chicago that the frontier and an era had ended, and the nation could look forward to the millennium of the twentieth century.

It is no coincidence that this journey was begun in earnest soon after the white American had elected to the presidency the first genuinely home-grown product of our culture to hold that high office. Even though it is now believed by some that Andrew Jackson was born aboard a ship bound for America, there is little doubt that democracy, white American style, was ushered in with his first Administration. Here was a man who understood the fundamental aspirations of his people, who saw clearly the task ahead and the obstacles which yet remained.

The Indian Removal Act which Jackson signed in 1830 was a truly representative piece of legislature—respresentative in the sense that it expressed the wishes of all white Americans who wanted to see their country move forward. Now Progress, great as it had undoubtedly been, would seem faltering and timid by comparison to what was begun in 1830. All the Indians, those visible reminders of the past and those bars to future progress, were to be removed west of the Mis-

sissippi River, where their wasteful nomadic
habits would trouble only a few. No matter now
that certain tribes like the Cherokee had ably
learned to walk the white man's road, had established schools, libraries, mills, churches, and shops
in the Old Southwest. Within five years after
Removal became official policy, the Cherokee
were started on the long walk westward, leaving
behind them their farms, stock, and mills to be
taken over by the nouveau conquistadores. They
joined the Ottawa, the Potawatomi, the Wyan-
dot, Shawnee, Kickapoo, Winnebago, Delaware,
Peoria, and the Miami. In Illinois, an old war
chief of the Sac and Fox tribe hoped for an alli-
ance between his people and the Winnebago and
Potawatomi tribes that would succeed in break-
ing the wave of the future. Black Hawk was even
deluded enough to imagine that the British would
help, but *that* tribe had already been crushed by
the American juggernaut and wanted no part
of any further schemes to oppose it. The result
was a hopeless, pathetic fifteen-week war during
which various heroes of white history—Abraham
Lincoln, Jefferson Davis, Zachary Taylor, and
Winfield Scott (he who would later tread Cortés's road to Mexico City)—collaborated to crush
the rebellion. Black Hawk and his confederate
chiefs were summoned to Washington where the
Great Father told them to be good and go West.
They did, and vanished.

There can be few clearer examples of the white
American's lost relationship to the natural world
than this policy of removal, for it was done in

callous disregard of the consequences of dumping thousands of alien Indians into an area the natural resources of which had provided abundant support for the tribes living there. But these resources were not, as both reds and whites were to discover, inexhaustible, and the forced arrival of these displaced tribes produced immediate strains and upsets in the ecology that resulted in the warfare for which the Plains Indians became famous. Both man's understanding of his proper relationship to the earth and the loss of that understanding—the Garden of Eden myth—were reenacted in what Peter Farb has justly described as the "mopping-up" operations carried on from 1850 to 1890. This blood-soaked, disease-ridden, famine-stalked tragedy was played out against the backdrop of a region so overpoweringly beautiful in both its harsh and lush extremes as to dwarf into mockery the relentless antics of the dispossessors. Treaties were signed—and broken —for "as long as the grass shall grow," Indians swept into battles of foregone conclusions with whites, singing that it was a good day to die, for nothing lives long, "only the earth and the grass." But the whites weren't listening.

When the Sioux in Minnesota rose up and killed as many as five hundred whites in 1862 and left a region fifty miles by two hundred miles barren of inhabitants, the nation was shocked. Then the whites gathered themselves together for a final assault which would make safe and sure the reign of happiness and white prosperity. Heroes of the Civil War were elevated to positions of central command of the operations. One of them, William Tecumseh Sherman (the middle name was to become grimly ironic in the next few decades), responded in approved military fashion to the depredations of the Sioux. "We must act with vindictive earnestness against the Sioux," he said, "even to their extermination, men, women and children. Nothing else will reach the root of this case." And to his brother John, United States Senator from Ohio, he wrote a contemplated assessment of the situation: "The more we can kill this year, the less will have to be killed the next war, for the more I see of these Indians the more convinced I am that all have to be killed or maintained as a species of pauper." Rarely has history afforded us an example of such effective carrying-out of orders.

Another hero, Philip Sheridan, is credited by Ralph K. Andrist with the original remark about "good Indians." At Fort Cobb, Indian Territory, a Comanche named Turtle Dove introduced himself to the general with the humble self-attribution that he was a "good Indian." "The only good Indians I know," the general returned, "are dead."

Such remarks make clearer than reams of official documents could what the real operating procedure was to be in the Plains campaigns. It was to be extermination, pure and simple, for the cause was holy, the provocations many, and the army mighty. Americans have always prided themselves on being able to achieve anything to which they dedicated themselves, and the extension of white rule across the length of the continent represented just such a communal dedication. Nothing—not the destruction of men, women, children, ponies, bison, grass, the very land itself—was permitted to arrest the machine-like operation, and if some of the village cleanups (like that at Sand Creek in 1864) were pretty bloody, these were but the inevitable hardships of making the continent. The whites proved better able to bear them than the Indians.

There were, of course, atrocities on both sides during the Long Death, but as Andrist has observed (and Herman Melville long before him) the supposed gap between the savage and the civilized often narrowed so that one was indistinguishable from the other. If anything, the whites showed greater ingenuity in their killing and mutilating than the Indians for whom such activities were presumed to be second nature. No Indian, for example, would have thought of the antics of certain white residents of Montana who cut off the heads of slain Indians, pickled the ears in whiskey, boiled the skin from the skulls, and then inscribed the bleached bones with such witticisms as "I am on the reservation at last."

So it went, onward to its relentless conclusion, through dozens of random massacres like the Fetterman Fight where the Sioux rubbed out eighty whites in forty-five minutes; the battle of the Washita where Custer earned the praise of whites and the undying enmity of reds by surprising Black Kettle's friendly camp, killing perhaps as many as a hundred Indians and eight hundred seventy-five ponies; the celebrated Battle of the Little Big Horn where the massed forces of Sioux and Cheyenne overran Custer and his portion of the Seventh Cavalry (a contemporary account by a Cheyenne who fought there says that many of the soldiers shot each other to avoid capture). But the next year (1877) it was really all over on the Plains. Andrist writes that as

> 1877 ended, in all the Great Plains, from Canada south, there was no longer a free tribe or a "wild" Indian. It had not taken long; in 1840 the boundary of the permanent Indian Country had been completed and the Great Plains were to belong forever to the Indians. A mere thirty-seven years later every solemn promise had been broken and no bit of ground large enough to be buried in remained to any Indian that could not—and probably would—be arbitrarily taken from him without warning.

By 1883 the destruction of the once limitless herds of bison which had roamed the Plains was virtually complete. It had long been an article of faith with Sherman and Sheridan that the quickest way to insure the destruction of the Indian was to destroy his sources of livelihood. As part of such a plan and as an earlier version of defoliation, the army started huge grass fires to burn off the forage for both the bison and the Indian ponies. In 1871 a new technological wrinkle, one of the many inventions which make the nineteenth century the preeminent century of Progress, made the wholesale slaughter of bison even more attractive a notion: the perfection of a process whereby excellent leather could be made from tanned buffalo hide. It was the buffalo, as George Bent recalled, and the horse that made the Cheyenne (and the other Plains tribes) "one of the proudest and most independent men that ever lived." Now that way of life, its men, its animals, was gone forever, and it remained only for the whites to tie up the loose ends in California to complete the whole process. In 1848 when gold was discovered in that area and it was annexed as a state, there were approximately one hundred thousand Indians there; by 1859 we had whittled that figure down to about thirty thousand; and by the turn of the century there were only fifteen thousand of the race once described by a righteous devotee of the white American way as "A set of miserable, dirty, lousy, blanketed, thieving, lying, sneaking, murdering, graceless, faithless, gut-eating skunks as the Lord ever permitted to infect the earth, and whose immediate and final extermination all men, except Indian agents and traders, should pray for." The prayers were answered.

II

A small, almost incidental step in this march of Progress was the subjugation and virtual annihilation of the Apache tribes of the Southwest. It was late and it was limited to the present states of Arizona and New Mexico with tedious campaigns into Old Mexico, but it was bloody and it produced more than its share of heroes, villains, and fools.

It will be recalled that Castañeda had mentioned the Apache in his chronicle of Coronado's parched peregrination across the deserts of the Southwest, but the reference was one of curiosity only. By 1600, however, the Apache were more than curiosities: they were threats to the process of colonization that the Spaniards had begun in the area.

These fierce, swift nomads enter the history of the Southwest like Goths, raiding, killing, and moving on. They came down from northwest Canada into the deserts and kept pushing south down into the Sierra Madres and the present states of Sonora and Chihuahua. The Spaniards found them terrible enemies, impossible to deal with in the approved Cortés manner: they hit and disappeared into the trackless mountains. The Apache were in fact guerrillas, a style of warfare not much in favor with imperialists, but quite necessary to their adversaries. A later guerrilla leader, Ché Guevara, would find considerable inspiration in reading of the tactics of Geronimo who had learned the arts of the quick hit and immediate disappearance from his forefathers.

By the time the white Americans were declaring their independence from *their* imperialist oppressors, the Spaniards had been at war with these red guerrillas for over a century—a century of raids, killings, punitive expeditions, isolated murders, despoiled pack trains, bodies rotting in the sun or frozen like cordwood in the high mountains. Now they began a determined drive destined to push the Apache northward out of Mexico into areas where they were attacked by their hereditary enemies, the Comanche. Caught in such an accidental pincers movement, the Apache dwindled in numbers but not in toughness. They established their domains in New Mexico and Arizona and still ranged in small parties through the northern tip of Mexico—so much so that by 1840 the state of Chihuahua was offering a bounty of one hundred dollars for a male Apache scalp and fifty for a female.

By this time the Hispanic wave of Western Progress had spent itself; the Spaniards had succeeded in fighting these Apache to a standoff, but if Western Civilization were to extend its rule throughout the New World, it would have to be the white Americans who finished the task. With faltering hands the Spanish passed the torch of our great tradition to the Americans in 1848 with the Treaty of Guadalupe Hidalgo, Article Eleven of which stated that from there on the Americans would take care of the Apache. Like other treaties the whites signed concerning the Indian, this one proved false. Three years later the Apache killed an estimated two hundred citizens in the state of Sonora alone and ran off about two thousand head of stock. And the year after that the Territorial Governor of New Mexico was writing to Secretary of State Daniel Webster that

Such is the daring of the Apache Indians that they openly attack our troops and force them to retreat or become victims of the scalping knife of the savages. Parties are being entirely cut off on the *Jornada* between Fort Conrad and Fort Fillmore; between these points an escort affords no longer any protection. The mail from San Elizario, which reached here last evening, was attacked on the *Jornada* by the Apaches; an escort of ten men was furnished them from Fort Conrad, of which one man was killed and two wounded in the encounter. The San Antonio mail is entirely cut off, to a man; the only remains found of the bloody struggle were the irons of the carriage and the bones of the men in charge. Such, Sir, are the reports which reach us from day to day, and it is a lamentable fact that they are increasing rapidly, to such an extent that if such outrages continue much longer, our territory, instead of becoming settled with an industrious and thriving population, will be left a howling wilderness, with no other inhabitants than the wolf, and the birds of prey, hovering over the mangled remains of our murdered countrymen.

The length of this excerpt is justified by its assumptions and the rhetoric by which these are expressed. Both are classics of the time and situation.

Who were these scalping savages whom white America had agreed to suppress when Mexico had to admit it couldn't? Beyond and beneath the assumptions about the virtues of settlements, the industriousness of future populations, the godliness of farming as opposed to the sinful wastefulness of hunting and gathering, beneath the rhetoric of territorial governors and senators and the horror-provoking accounts of "depredations" (the favorite word to describe Indian attacks; also "massacre" to describe the killing by reds of two or more whites, while "fight" or "battle" describes the killing by whites of anywhere from two to a hundred reds)—beyond all this remarkably little was known—or is—about the Apache. If it had not been for the efforts of two anthropologists, Morris Opler and Grenville Goodwin, who interviewed hundreds of Apache at a time when the old ways were still remembered and the tribal history still intact, even less would have survived.

There are, or were, four distinct Apache tribes, the Chiricahua, the Mescalero, the Lipan, and the Jicarilla. Confusion often arises from the fact that each of these tribes is subdivided into bands and that these bands are further subdivided into local groups, or, in certain cases, clans. Moreover the various bands and local groups have been given a variety of names in the white literature about them. Thus a band of Chiricahua Apache inhabiting in pre-white days the area of southwestern New Mexico and the northernmost tip of Old Mexico have been called variously the Warm Springs Apache, the Ojo Caliente, Coppermine Apache, Mimbreños Apache, and Mogollones Apache. The Apache themselves refer to this people as the *čihéné*, or "Red Paint People." Of these tribes the toughest to tame (and the verb itself is significant) were the Chiricahua and for this reason and because of the colorfulness of one of their leaders, they have become synonymous in the popular imagination with all Apache.

The colorful leader, of course, is Geronimo who described himself as a born member of the Southern Chiricahua but seems to have grown up under the chieftainship of Mangus-Colorado of the Eastern Chiricahua. (The reader of Geronimo's autobiography will immediately experience the difficulty of sorting out the accepted divisions and subdivisions of the Chiricahua from Geronimo's recollection of tribal and band designations; the difficulty, I suspect is partly linguistic, since the autobiography is a translation of the old man's dictation and many Apache names simply do not yield to linguistic analysis.)

For apologists for the Indians, lovers of things Indian in general, and antiquarians with a sentimental bent, a study of the Chiricahua and their history and the career of Geronimo represents a real touchstone. Many such individuals will choose to concentrate upon the history and lore of other tribes like the Cheyenne, the Navaho, or the Sioux, none of which was ever as aggressive as the Chiricahua. But it is precisely for this reason that this latter tribe is so interesting. If we are to understand the true meaning of the cultural clash that resulted in the desetruction of the Indian, we must try to confront the realities of the situation—*all* of them. It might be tempting to dwell upon the more peaceable Indian tribes and then point the accusatory "liberal" finger at the whites, but this would not be true to the complexity of the clash. Warfare was a significant part of the cultures of almost all the tribes; men were honored for their skill as killers, even as we have our generals and war heroes; status came with success in war; and even the supposedly tranquil tribes had their ceremonies to celebrate the annihilation of enemies. To concentrate, then, on the Chiricahua Apache is to bring this aspect of red/white relations into sharp focus and thereby save ourselves from the inaccuracies which result in counterproductive orgies of racial self-hatred.

Let us be blunt. Let us say with respect to the wars between the white Americans and the Chiricahua that we are dealing with an irreconcilable conflict between an aggressive, war-minded colonizing group which could not tolerate differences and divergences from its rule and an aggressive and war-minded group of people for whom the raid was the most important and legitimate of tribal enterprises and for whom the war of vengeance was the inevitable consequence of the raid. Only when we understand the natures of the opposing cultures can we begin to ask what it might mean that one destroyed the other.

It is axiomatic that the way a person behaves, the way he feels and thinks, even the way he looks in body and dress, are products of his culture, and this is even more obviously true for smaller, nonliterate, homogeneous groups than for large, heterogeneous cultures like our own. From the beginning the Chiricahua raised their males to be strong, swift, deep-chested runners, rustlers of stock and raiders of pack trains, good hiders and dodgers, and implacable haters of non-tribal neighbors. Look through any collection of

photographs of the Apache and you will see looking out at you faces that neither give nor ask
quarter, faces broad and unsmiling (what indeed
was there to smile at?), set with eyes so deep and
hot that they appear almost glazed and strangely
milky, and still all these years later seem to scorch
the very pages they are printed on. (There is, in
fact, a very great deal to be learned about our
history in general and the white/red wars of the
last century by simply looking at photographs;
often the attributions are incorrect and the textual
material in general confused, but the faces of the
whites and the Indians and the circumstances of
the photographs themselves—often taken in photographers' studios with impossibly faked back-
grounds—have much to tell us about the deeply
human dimensions behind and beneath the facts
and figures of the battles.)

"As soon as I was old enough to know . . . I was
told who were our enemies," said an Apache, and
Geronimo himself tells the Chiricahua creation
myth in which one of the two culture heroes is
named "Killer of Enemies." Here is an Apache
father's advice to his son:

> My son, you know no one will help you in this
> world. You must do something. You run to that
> mountain and come back. That will make you
> strong. My son, you know no one is your
> friend, not even your sister, your father, or
> your mother. Your legs are your friends; your
> brain is your friend; your eyesight is your
> friend; your hair is your friend; your hands
> are your friends; you must do something with
> them. . . .

Some day you will be with people who are starving. You will have to get something for them. If you go somewhere, you must beat the enemy who are attacking you before they get over the hill. . . . Before they beat you, you must get in front of them . . . and bring them back dead. Then all the people will be proud of you. Then you will be the only man. Then all the people will talk about you. That is why I talk to you in this way.

He is telling his son that since the Apache live by raiding (or, if you are the one being raided, by "stealing") he must train himself in the arts of pursuit, ambush, and death; that death to the enemies is life to the Chircahua. So the boy enters a novitiate intended to produce at last just such a man as glares out at us from the photographs of old Geronimo. He learns to run four miles holding a mouthful of water without spilling or swallowing any (the Chiricahua, though they eventually acquired the horse sometime in the late eighteenth or early nineteenth century, always remained great runners, often traveling seventy miles or more a day on foot). He participates in wrestling tournaments with his peers to acquire toughness in hand-to-hand combat. He stands with three other boys on a flat plain and faces four others across an interval; all are armed with slings and rocks. The boys sling the rocks at each other and attempt to dodge them. The penalty for failure may be a broken bone or even death. When he has passed these tests he stands out once more against a line of boy adversaries, only this time all have bows and wooden, sharp-tipped arrows; they shoot at each other. Eventually there stands before you a young man, well trained in the arts of his profession, not big (a survey made in the late nineteenth century confirms one's impressions from the photographs that the Apache were rather short people; the average height of the men was five feet, six and one-half inches; the women averaged an even five feet), but looking like a steel- or bone-pointed missile, and hungering to be talked of for exploits in battle.

If this seems to be a lopsided view of Chiricahua culture, it may be only that *our* ethnocentrism suggests this, or it may be that the culture *was* lopsided. It is probably a little of both, and of course there is much more than this to the way the Chiricahua once lived and thought. But this was the center of their culture; it was the way they got their living. And *now*—especially now—perhaps one could say that this was a way of life, a culture, that could not and should not endure; that the stakes are now too high to allow one group of people to live by stealing from others and killing them when they retaliated. (But haven't the stakes always been too high? What could be higher than life and the loss of life itself?)

Does this mean then that it is necessary to destroy these people ruthlessly and to pen up on arid wastes the few survivors; to hand them shovels and hoes and tell them to turn into farmers overnight? Had they *nothing* of value, *nothing* to teach us?

The nineteenth-century white American mind dutifully received the message from Western Civilization that, yes, the Apache would have to go; that, yes, they must be penned up on reservations to learn progressive ways; and that, no, there was nothing worth salvaging from this wolfish bunch of thieves.

But there was.

The Chiricahua, indeed all the Apache, had the priceless inheritance of those who live so close to the natural world that they cannot ever forget that they are a part of it and that it is a part of them.

Here is the approved Chiricahua method for the disposal of afterbirth: the mother wraps it up in the piece of cloth or blanket upon which she has knelt during labor and places it in the branches of a nearby fruit-bearing bush or tree. This is done because "the tree comes to life every year, and they want the life of this child to be renewed like the life in the tree." Before the bundle is placed in the branches the midwife blesses it, saying, "May the child live and grow up to see you bear fruit many times." Thereafter that place is sacred to the child and to his parents. The child is told where he was born, and if possible the parents take him back to that spot a few years later and roll him on the ground to the four directions. Even adults, when they chance to be once again in the area where they were born, will roll themselves to the cardinal points in symbolic communication with the giant wheel that turns everything with it, "whose center is everywhere and whose circumference is nowhere." This is why Geronimo begins the story of his life with a careful description of the place of his birth and why, at the end of that story, he says that the Apache are steadily dying because they have not been allowed to return to their homelands. To the Indian mind, a man's attachment to his homeland was not a romantic nostrum but a vital necessity; a man sickened and eventually died— a whole people might die away—if cut off from the life-source of the land itself. And so Geronimo, that "bloodthirsty savage," ends his autobiography with a plea which has the unmistakable dignity of profound conviction: he asks the Great Father, Theodore Roosevelt, to return him and his people to their Arizona homelands.

That plea was lost upon a people bent upon forgetting that they "could never have enough of nature." It seemed to the whites then that they had already had too much of it and that one of the central glories of the American experience had been just this taming of nature, turning the howling wilderness into a garden and then into a City on a Hill, a beacon light for the Old World. So the Apache never got back home.

But before they were subdued they made one of the great stands in the whole sorry history of dispossession. The combination of the culture traits of war/raid and abiding attachment to land enabled Geronimo and the Chiricahua to avoid a final surrender for more than a decade. It was a bloody decade, one filled with lies and broken promises on both sides, but if one can abstract raw courage and fierce dedication to traditional beliefs from military activities, then one might admire Geronimo, Naiche (Natchez), and their small band of Chiricahua even as one might admire Black Hawk and the Sac and Fox, or Captain Jack and his Modoc, or Chief Joseph and the Nez Percé, or Dull Knife and the homeward-bound Cheyenne whom the army tried to starve into submission, but who resisted until the last warrior charged the troops with nothing but his war cry and an empty revolver.

Originally the Apache seemed friendly to the white Americans, but this was probably because neither represented a threat to the other. This was in 1807, when Zeb Pike was stumbling around lost in the desert and probably glad to see some other people out there. Relations were bound to worsen with increased contact, considering the principals involved. In 1837 two white traders killed an Apache chief, but widespread trouble was averted.

It could not be averted after October 1860, from which time we can date the Apache wars ending only when Geronimo and Naiche surrendered the remnants of their band in the late summer of 1886.

In that October of 1860 a man named Ward beat his half-breed son so savagely that the boy ran away. When Ward sobered up he told everybody that the Chiricahua chief Cochise had stolen the boy and some stock as well. A punitive expedition was mounted by the soldiers, but before they could chastise Cochise he came in with his head men to protest his innocence.

Once the whites had these Chiricahua inside the parley tent, however, they could not resist the temptation to capture them. A ring of soldiers closed up around the tent while, inside, Cochise was informed that he and his men would be held prisoners until the missing boy and the stock were returned. When he heard this, Cochise whipped out his knife, slashed a hole in the tent, and leapt through it. The waiting soldiers outside were so surprised to see this tall Indian in their midst that they parted ranks like the Red Sea, and Cochise escaped. Soon after, he captured three whites as hostages and set about the business of long-distance negotiations to secure the release of his own men.

But the whites weren't bargaining, and in a rage at their stubbornness, treachery, and ignorance, Cochise dragged one of the hostages to death behind his horse while a detachment of soldiers looked on. Later, still unable to get his men back, the chief had the other two hostages killed. In reprisal the whites hanged the six innocent Chiricahua in February 1861. The Cochise wars were on, and for ten years the chief made whites in Arizona and New Mexico wish they had questioned that Mr. Ward more closely. (The runaway boy, by the way, was Mickey Free who later became a scout in the final Chiricahua campaigns.)

Whereas on the Plains the coming of the Civil War—another successful attempt by the dominant culture to stamp out differences wherever they appeared—had meant a temporary if incomplete relief from the relentless pressure of the troops, for the Chiricahua things during the war years were even more hazardous. Both Confederate and Union forces were in their area. Both sides offered bounties for Apache scalps, but the contemplated Confederate strategy against the Indians was somewhat more savage than that of their adversaries. Writing instructions to the commander of the Arizona Guards in 1862, Confederate Governor John R. Baylor said:

> I learn from Lieutenant J. J. Jackson that Indians have been in your post for the purpose of making a treaty. The Congress of the Confederate States has passed a law declaring extermination to all hostile Indians. You will therefore use all means to persuade the Apaches or any tribe to come in for the purpose of making peace, and when you get them together kill all the grown Indians and take the children prisoners and sell them to defray the expense of killing the Indians. Buy whisky and such other goods as may be necessary for the Indians and I will order vouchers given to cover the amount expended. Leave nothing undone to insure success, and have a sufficient number of men around to allow no Indian to escape.

Fortunately for the Apache, higher Confederate command found this plan too brutal, and it was never put into practice, though it was suggested that at such future time as was practical the Apache be "legally enslaved." Such a suggestion

must have seemed altogether natural to South-
erners.

In January 1863, Mangus-Colorado was
treacherously taken prisoner and assassinated in
what Geronimo calls the "greatest wrong ever
done to the Indians." (Like many Indians, Geronimo assumed that "Indian" and his tribe's
name were synonymous; in the case of some tribes
there is but one word for both the tribal name
and the word meaning human beings.) Though
this blow for Progress was struck by the Grand
Army of the Republic, surely the Confederates
would have approved its style which is amply
described in Geronimo's autobiography. Other
similar acts of dishonesty—such as treating the
Apache to a gift of pinole nuts seasoned with
strychnine—continued during the war years, but
at the war's end the final solution to the Apache
problem was not in sight.

It might have emerged in a less grim fashion
than it finally did had the Chiricahua and other
Apache groups been given the generous reservations and hunting preserves that Thomas Jeffords
and a few other farseeing whites had requested
for them. It was Jeffords who at last won the
respect of the great Cochise and cooled the fires
of his hatred so much that the chief was finally
willing to bring his bands in near a reservation at
Fort Bowie. Other Apache groups had already
agreed to settle on reservations, but what happened at Fort Grant, Arizona, in the same year
that Cochise and his Chiricahua laid down their

arms cannot have inspired them with much confidence.

At the end of April 1871, a group of one hundred and forty-six assassins marched from Tucson and fell upon the sleeping camp of the Arivaipa Apache at peace on the Camp Grant Reservation. Papago Indians, Mexicans, and leading white citizens from Tucson stole in among the wickiups and began the silent butchering with heavy clubs and knives. A few minutes later when the camp became aroused, rifles did the work, and in within a half hour the job was finished: an estimated one hundred and eight Apache killed, only eight of whom were men, the bulk of the males being off hunting. Later a trial was arranged for those implicated in the "fight"; a jury deliberated twenty minutes before returning an acquittal.

Can we better understand, then, that deep distrust of all whites which so clearly characterizes Geronimo, Victoria (or spelled Victorio), Naiche (or spelled Natchez), Whoa (also Who and Juh), and the Chiricahua during the 1870s and '80s? And of all the distrustful, the intransigent, the wild, the worst from the white point of view was Geronimo because he was the best from the standpoint of Chiricahua culture. Among a people whose way of life was the raid and for whom the war of vengeance was the inevitable aftermath, Geronimo rose to prominence as a raider and warrior. Among a people who worshiped the land, Geronimo's attachment to his territory became legendary.

So successful in raiding and warring did Ge-

ronimo become that he can best be described
within Chiricahua culture as a war shaman, that
is, a kind of unofficial priest or healer (as Peter
Farb has it) whose special area of competence is
the planning and execution of raids and wars.
Now, in Chiricahua culture shamanism abounds,
and the possession of a ceremony, big or small,
makes one a shaman. But in times of strife the
man who knew ceremonies for effectively dealing
with enemies would be particularly important.
It is clear that, for the Chiricahua, strife was a
way of life, but with the white Americans pressing them throughout the '60s and '70s tension and
strife rose to new levels, and so did Geronimo.
With the Chiricahua way of life threatened as it
had never been before, this man came forward
to a position of leadership at least equal to that
of a hereditary chief, which he himself was not.

Geronimo's way was the *old* Chiricahua way,
and nothing he saw in the behavior or actions of
whites convinced him that Cochise was right in
bringing his bands in to the reservation. Certainly
he saw nothing very attractive in the style of life
which the whites had marked out for the Chiricahua once they got them on the reservation: the
Chiricahua had never been very extensive or serious farmers, probably because they moved
about so much; now they were to be exclusively
farmers. (Some Chiricahua whom Morris Opler
interviewed claimed that the tribe had never
farmed until the coming of the whites, though
Geronimo says in his autobiography that they
used to do some planting when he was a child.)

The raid and the war of vengeance were now to be ended; a Chiricahua could not beat his wife for misdeeds, nor could he cut off the end of her nose if he found her unfaithful; nor could he even make tiswin, the maize-based beer of which he was so fond. In short, the Chiricahua was to become a pretend white man without being able to share fully in the white man's culture.

These things went hard with the Chiricahua, and especially the men, but they went harder with Geronimo than with anyone else, again, perhaps because he was himself the perfection of the Chiricahua way. Others, less perfect—or with clearer vision as history tells us now—preferred to make these difficult accommodations, and there is enough evidence to indicate that Geronimo was both hated and feared by some of his people because of his uncompromising behavior. In his autobiography he tells us as much when he recounts his early days as a warrior leading expeditions down into Old Mexico, but in the '70s and '80s he used tricks, lies, and sometimes outright kidnapping to get his people to continue to fight against the whites—and this he did *not* choose to tell his white editor.

In April 1876, Geronimo led a band of Chiricahua off the Fort Bowie reservation in the first of his major transgressions against the new white way. For almost exactly a year he and Victoria remained what the whites would call "at large," which is to say that they lived the old Chiricahua way, but with a new focus of venom—the whites who seemed more determined to rub them out than the Mexicans ever had been.

Pressed hard and hemmed in by troops, Geronimo and Victoria came in near Fort Thomas in April 1877, and surrendered themselves to Apache Agent John P. Clum in a very tense scene during which only the presence of a large squad of Clum's Apache police prevented the hostiles from killing their presumptive captors. Only when Geronimo saw that the odds—his own people in police uniforms—were against him did he pull his thumb back from the hammer of his rifle and allow that he was willing to talk.

The substance of the talk was that Geronimo and his band would have to come in to the San Carlos Reservation and learn to be good agrarians. After all, John Locke and Jefferson both had said that a man only becomes human when he takes something out of the natural state and converts it to his own use; that is how property became private, how men grew rich, and nations prospered. It was assumed to be the final proof of the Apache's subhuman nature that he could not understand the notion of upward mobility through the accumulation of wealth. The agents, watching the Indians poke listlessly at the reservation soil, despaired of ever teaching them that love of property that would mean civilization. The situation is so bitterly ironic even at this remove that one cannot trust oneself to play with it. Here was a group of people whose attachment to land had made them defend it with their life's blood, and riding herd on them was a group whose only attachment to land was what they could rape out of it. Considering the white Americans' uses of this country's natural resources during the last century, I do not think that is too strong a statement.

Geronimo learned to grow watermelons, the agents said, and like all good Indians he seemed proud of this accomplishment and eager to show visitors to his small patch. But Geronimo was not a good Indian in Sheridan's sense, or in any other that the whites were prepared to understand. In September 1881, he jumped the reservation again and headed toward the Sierra Madre Mountains, those mountains of legend and literature, where the Apache had always been safe from pursuit and capture.

Since this is history and not a novel it can't turn out that Geronimo and his band remained free in these mountains. Even as we might wish this, we know that is not what happened. General George Crook, the most successful tracker of Apache the whites ever put into the field, found the hostiles and got them to agree to return, though he gave them a two-month extension to round up the small groups scattered through the crags. It was almost a year later when Geronimo showed up at the border, and he announced his coming by a mile-high cloud of dust rising from under the hooves of cattle and horses he had stolen during these months from the Mexican. If the whites placed such a premium on riches, he was at least going back to their world well supplied

with these. Alas, they were all taken from him
at San Carlos.

Now it was even tougher to live on the reservation than it had been before: it was over-
crowded; there were serious intertribal antagon-
isms; and as for Geronimo, he was a man with a
reputation. Still, as he played at farming, he
schemed for a way to get his people together
again for a large break that might destroy the
reservation system forever. As usual in situations
of this sort, the whites were playing right into the
warriors' hands: they were ever ready to give Indians cause to revolt by being utterly ruthless in
their attempts to destroy the tribal culture. In
this instance it was the issues of tiswin drinking
and wife-beating that brought about the confron-
tation Geronimo had been seeking.

In the middle of May 1885, with the situation
at San Carlos tense over these issues, Geronimo
told Naiche and another chief, Chihuahua, that
Lieutenant Britton Davis and Chatto, a friendly
Chiricahua chief, had been murdered and that the
whites were going to arrest these three for the
murders. In fact, the murders had never taken
place, though Geronimo had instructed two warriors to commit them when the break from the
reservation had been made. Geronimo's plan
worked, and the three men and a sizable band
left the reservation and traveled toward Old
Mexico. But as an indication of how the tide was
running, it must be recorded here that when
Naiche and Chihuahua discovred how they had

been tricked into this act of defiance, they came near to killing Geronimo.

Again General Crook was sent into the field, and again he found the Chiricahua after an incredible campaign which ended—or at the time *seemed* to have ended—with Crook's famous conference with Geronimo and the chiefs at El Cañon de los Embudos, March 25 and 27, 1886. The conference became famous not only because it was thought to have represented the final capitulation of the man who had come to be in the white American mind everybody's Bad Injun, but because it was attended by a photographer and a reporter, like other modern-day peace conferences, which we can now look back upon and wonder what in all that business and paraphernalia went wrong.

C. S. Fly, one of the West's most intrepid photographers, made the trip to the cañon and brought back a series of remarkable pictures, the best known of which shows the whites seated in an open-ended circle with their quarry, Geronimo, squatting in the center, looking small against these big bearded men. From the accidental composition of the photograph, however, you would think he was a meteorite just dropped into their midst. In the background lurk the armed figures of his Chiricahua warriors.

In terms of actual negotiations it was not much of a conference. The Chiricahua were well supplied with guns, ammunition, and horses, all of which they had stolen since they jumped the reservation. But they were vastly outnumbered, they were hungry, and the people were getting tired of running. All except Geronimo. After Chihuahua and Naiche had come forward on the twenty-seventh to make rather abject surrender speeches to Crook, the old warrior himself, no chief and so not able to really speak for anyone but himself, came forward and in a few simple words gave up:

> Two or three words are enough. I have little to say. I surrender to you. We are all comrades, all one family, all one band. What the others say I say also. I give myself up to you. Do with me what you please. I surrender. Once I moved about like the wind. Now I surrender to you and that is all.

That was all. The Chiricahua had been taken, and General Crook left Fort Bowie with a satisfied heart. The Chiricahua retired to their camp a little way up in the hills, and the soldiers settled down to rest for the trip back to civilization.

None reckoned, however, with one of those inevitable harbingers of civilization, a man named Tribolet (or Tribollet) who had come out to the conference with a wagon full of whiskey and a tent to sell it in. The evidence of the next morning plainly showed that Geronimo and Naiche had bought heavily of the good merchant's rot-gut, doctored with tobacco and assorted trash to give it an authentic bite. Not only had Tribolet sold the Indians this stuff, but he had told them that once they were back on United States soil, they would be shot down by the troops.

The combination of the bad liquor, fears of ambush, and general distrust of whites proved far stronger than the handshakes with Crook of the day before, and when the caravan started off on March 28—the soldiers in the lead, the Chiricahua following—Geronimo, Naiche, and a party of thirty-eight (some say thirty-nine) men, women, and children slipped away into the hills. The main party continued on, but Crook had lost his biggest catch.

One can perfectly imagine without the aid of official documents how Crook's immediate superior, Philip Sheridan, reacted to the loss of Geronimo. Crook resigned, and General Nelson A. Miles replaced him with orders to run the little band—already it was doing its full share of killing and looting—into the ground. A huge pursuit force was sent out with orders to kill or capture, preferably the former. This time there was to be no treating with the hostiles.

Miles gave effective command of this latest expedition to Captain H. W. Lawton of the Fourth Cavalry, who in his turn wisely employed several old friends of Geronimo, now serving the whites as scouts and trackers. Only the Apache could track the Apache into Old Mexico and its mountains.

At that it took almost five months before Geronimo came in near Fronteras in Sonora to ask for peace. There were no terms offered, and Geronimo was hardly in a position to bargain for any: the people had simply had it. They were tired, ragged, starving, and finally their will to resist had been broken. This is the inevitable end of any culture clash between a people with a huge numerical and technological superiority and a tiny tribe essentially pretechnological. If the large culture really puts its resources to work, harasses its quarry ceaselessly, and is encumbered with no scruples as to the treatment of its adversaries, then it will ineluctably break the spirit of the resisters. It will reduce them to that species of permanent paupers originally envisioned by William Tecumseh Sherman. Who can deny that this ability is a part of the American genius, that Americans can do this, and have done it?

When Geronimo and Naiche surrendered for the last time on September 4, 1886, and a few days later were put aboard a train to Florida, they were headed for a life of pauperdom even if they did not know it. The other once-hostile Chiricahua had already been put aboard another train for Florida, leaving behind them at the railroad station their personal belongings, their horses, and their dogs, some of these latter forlornly running after the departing train and going on for twenty miles down the tracks. The train, that symbol of Progress, which had cut its way westward, split the bison herd in two, and joined the coasts of a continent, was now bearing into alien grounds the last remnants of the human barriers who had once for a brief moment in history thought to oppose something they never really understood.

So now it was done, the great adventure of "making the continent" was over, and Americans could, if they had wished, have looked back at the turn of the century over the way that they had come. They would have seen then a line of tawdry, jerry-built towns, stringing out like discarded plowlines from the east; towns which still retained some of the raw, whiskey-soaked, bullet-riddled, privy-stinking marks of their low and recent origins; towns sitting in the midst of now-empty spaces, huddled under the burlesque shadows of county courthouses, those gaping, empty, pathetically public monuments to the vanity and expectations of the settlers. They might still have seen on the wide plains the moldering bones of the bison who once ate the grass that was now mostly gone, too, as the whole, huge middle region turned into a dust bowl. But the rotting carcasses of the bison had sunk back into the earth and even most of the bones had been gathered up by the last scavengers and sold for glue as if they could thereby make the whole thing stick together. They would not have seen the Indians unless they were to look toward those dry, savagely eroded plots upon which the red man had been compelled to die. The Chiricahua by that time were safely on their postage stamp at Fort Sill, Oklahoma, after eight years in Florida and Alabama. Twenty-five percent of the tribe had died in that unfamiliar climate but all were now thoroughly domesticated.

In the minds of the white Americans the nineteenth century had been the century of Progress, that period when all the inventions, the expertise, and the muscle had opened wide the way to the millennium. Though there was something sad about the finish of the westering, and though there was a "line of old men along the shore hating the ocean because it stopped them," it was clear then that that giant process and everything it entailed had been but a step in the march of Progress. It had been great and glorious, but Progress was something bigger than any single movement in it.

Now it is no longer very clear to us what the Winning of the West meant, because it is no longer clear what Progress itself means. Up to our eyeballs in the indestructible junk that the unstoppable machine of Progress daily spews out— the aluminum containers, plastic retainers, synthetic foods and fibers of all kinds—breathing stertorously the pestiferous atmosphere of our waste-clogged continent, we must wonder seriously whether our forward progress is not a death march. Our probes into space, which we are now also littering with aimlessly whizzing bits of metal, cannot solve the problem; at best they provide but a temporary and dangerous illusion of yet another frontier to subdue. But they do not solve the question of Progress by accelerating it.

Out of the eyes of that incorruptible Chiricahua leader glares a challenge to our cherished notions of ourselves, of Western Civilization, and of the relentless energy which for centuries has nerved it. Geronimo and his people were unwilling sacrifices to Progress, but we are, too. The men and women strapped to business machines and those in assembly lines are equally victims with Geronimo, Black Kettle, and the Cherokee. And those of us who think we have escaped such dehumanizing routines are no less victims in virtually every aspect of our daily lives, in the food we eat, the air we breathe, the waters we drink and play in. All of us, red and white, have been sacrificed to Progress, and our continent has become but a morsel being steadily devoured by those huge metallic jaws that not so long ago ground up the Indian exceeding small.

So the last words of Thoreau continue to haunt us as they remind us of a certain race of men, less progressive, less ambitious, but no less human and quite possibly just a bit more so. Those words remind us that this race of men had an important lesson to teach us about man's proper and necessary relationship to his natural environment. We might also learn from their passing that no enduring order can be founded on the refuse piles of things—men, animals, land —which made way for it.

Perhaps it is not too late to learn this, though it is clearly too late for the Indians. The destruction of cultures is an irreversible process, and since we have largely destroyed most of their cultures, the Indians will have to develop new ones if they are to emancipate themselves from that pauperdom to which we so callously relegated them.

But we can still learn something from the old Indian ways of life. Despite our best efforts there remains a small but supremely valuable body of aboriginal literature, not the least of which are the Indian autobiographies. Almost all of these are mutilated, and most of them were transcribed by the conquering whites, but despite these handicaps there speaks a single voice through them all—that same large voice that echoes through the surviving myths, tales, and poetry of the Indians. That voice is the voice of a man with his feet planted like roots in the soil of his Mother Earth, his hands open to receive the seasonal blessings of wind, sun, and rain, his heart reverent in the presence of a wildness he knows is unfathomed because essentially unfathomable.

We need to read these life stories of the Indians, but we need first to learn how to read them. When we do learn that we will find that they are not telling us to return to the breechclout, to torture tests of endurance, or to the mutilation of social aberrants. Still less are they telling us to live by stealing and murdering. But they are a way, perhaps one of the few we have left ourselves , of *re*learning both our limitations and our excellences. As Americans there could be no more appropriate place for us to begin this new kind of progress than with the stories of a race of men which has well-nigh vanished because we have forgotten these things.

A NOTE ON THE TEXT

GERONIMO told the story of his life in 1905–6 to Asa (Ace) Daklugie, the son of Whoa (Who, Juh), a hostile chief who fought with Geronimo in the last campaigns and who drowned in a stream outside of Casa Grandes, Mexico, in 1886 (he had gotten drunk on mescal during a peace mission). Daklugie, who had received some education from the whites, translated the story for S. M. Barrett, a white who was then Superintendent of Education in nearby Lawton, Oklahoma.

During the storytelling sessions Geronimo would range freely over the events of his life in the characteristic Indian manner. This manner consists of telling *only that which seems to the teller important and telling it in the fashion and the order which seems to him appropriate*. I emphasize this because it is clear that certain rearrangements of the materials would make a more coherent narrative. Yet this would not be the aboriginal style of extended narratives, and so it would be false to make such changes. I have resisted the temptation, and Geronimo's narrative stands as Barrett published it. I have, however, deleted some of Barrett's obviously superfluous material: in his introduction the narration of his dealings with the War Department and in the body his account of Apache/white warfare in the nineteenth century.

As to the accuracy of the whole, let us say to begin with that Geronimo, for reasons of his own, did not choose to tell Barrett everything. He was, after all, still a prisoner of war, and he was a bitter man who regretted to the end of his life that he had surrendered to Miles rather than fighting it out in the mountains. Considering his treatment in subsequent years, one cannot much blame him. At any rate, there are numerous gaps and omissions in his narrative, and wherever possible I have tried to supply the relevant factual data in footnotes followed by my initials (FWT). In some cases, particularly those events before Geronimo came to the attention of whites, it is simply impossible to comment on what Geronimo says. I have left the majority of Barrett's footnotes (followed by his initials) as they originally occurred even though these are occasionally inaccurate. It seems to me useful to see how much more incomplete white knowledge of Indians was then than it is now, even though we do not know nearly as much as we should.

As for Geronimo's life in captivity, I think his own words tell us more than any other source might how he felt about his treatment. It is interesting, however, that just as he was the supreme embodiment of the Chiricahua way of life, so he became a very shrewd capitalist when the white way was forced upon him. In fact, he took on all the trappings of the white man's civilization, becoming a farmer, a member of the Dutch Reformed Church, a Sunday school teacher, and a tireless promoter of himself, hawking photographs, bows and arrows at various fairs and expositions. He was one Indian who exploited the exploiters better than they could him.

Geronimo died February 17, 1909, in the military hospital at Fort Sill. Frank Lockwood reports that he interviewed an official of the Dutch Reformed Church who said that a few days before his death Geronimo had gone to nearby Lawton to sell one of the bows he was always making. While there he got drunk with the money from the sale and returning "home" fell out of his buggy and lay all night on the road in a freezing rain. He was discovered the next day and taken to the hospital, where he died. By his own reckoning Geronimo was about eighty. He died a prisoner of war.

INTRODUCTORY

I FIRST met Geronimo in the summer of 1904, when I acted for him as interpreter of English into Spanish, and vice versa, in selling a war bonnet. After that he always had a pleasant word for me when we met, but never entered into a general conversation with me until he learned that I had once been wounded by a Mexican. As soon as he was told of this, he came to see me and expressed freely his opinion of the average Mexican and his aversion to all Mexicans in general.

I invited him to visit me again, which he did, and upon his invitation, I visited him at his tepee in the Fort Sill Military reservation.

In the summer of 1905, Dr. J. M. Greenwood, superintendent of schools at Kansas City, Missouri, visited me, and I took him to see the chief. Geronimo was quite formal and reserved until Dr. Greenwood said, "I am a friend of General Howard, whom I have heard speak of you." "Come," said Geronimo, and led the way to a shade, had seats brought for us, put on his war bonnet, and served watermelon à l'Apache (cut in big chunks), while he talked freely and cheerfully. When we left he gave us a pressing invitation to visit him again.

In a few days the old chief came to see me and asked about "my father." I said, "You mean the old gentleman from Kansas City—he has returned to his home." "He is your father?" said Geronimo. "No," I said, "my father died twenty-five years ago, Dr. Greenwood is only my friend." After a moment's silence the old Indian spoke again, this time in a tone of voice intended to carry conviction, or at least to allow no further discussion. "Your natural father is dead, this man has been your friend and adviser from youth. By adoption *he is your father*. Tell him he is welcome to come to my home at any time." It was of no use to explain any more, for the old man had determined not to understand my relation to Dr. Greenwood except in accordance with Indian customs, and I let the matter drop.

In the latter part of that summer I asked the old chief to allow me to publish some of the things he had told me, but he objected, saying, however, that if I would pay him, and if the officers in charge did not object, he would tell me the whole story of his life.[1] I immediately called at the fort (Fort Sill) and asked the officer in charge, Lieutenant Purington, for permission to write the life of Geronimo. I was promptly informed that

[1] Typical of Geronimo's behavior in the late years of his captivity. He had learned the hard way how much money counted in the white man's culture and would do little for the whites without pay. (FWT)

the privilege would not be granted. Lieutenant Purington explained to me the many depredations committed by Geronimo and his warriors, and the enormous cost of subduing the Apaches, adding that the old Apache deserved to be hanged rather than spoiled by so much attention from civilians. A suggestion from me that our government had paid many soldiers and officers to go to Arizona and kill Geronimo and the Apaches, and that they did not seem to know how to do it, did not prove very gratifying to the pride of the regular army officer, and I decided to seek elsewhere for permission. Accordingly I wrote to President Roosevelt that here was an old Indian who had been held a prisoner of war for twenty years and had never been given a chance to tell his side of the story, and asked that Geronimo be granted permission to tell for publication, in his own way, the story of his life, and that he be guaranteed that the publication of his story would not affect unfavorably the Apache prisoners of war. By return mail I received word that the authority had been granted. In a few days I received word from Fort Sill that the President had ordered the officer in charge to grant permission as requested. An interview was requested that I might receive the instructions of the War Department. When I went to Fort Sill the officer in command handed me a brief, which constituted my instructions.

Early in October I secured the services of an educated Indian, Asa Daklugie, son of Whoa, chief of the Nedni Apaches, as interpreter, and the work of compiling the book began.

Geronimo refused to talk when a stenographer was present, or to wait for corrections or questions when telling the story. Each day he had in mind what he would tell and told it in a very clear, brief manner. He might prefer to talk at his own tepee, at Asa Daklugie's house, in some mountain dell, or as he rode in a swinging gallop across the prairie; whenever his fancy led him, there he told whatever he wished to tell and no more.[2] On the day that he first gave any portion of his autobiography he would not be questioned about any details, nor would he add another word, but simply said, "Write what I have spoken," and left us to remember and write the story without one bit of assistance. He would agree, however, to come on another day to my study, or any place designated by me, and listen to the reproduction (in Apache) of what had been told, and at such times would answer all questions or add information wherever he could be convinced that it was necessary.

He soon became so tired of book making that he would have abandoned the task but for the fact that he had agreed to tell the complete story. When he once gives his word, nothing will turn him from fulfilling his promise. A very striking illustration of this was furnished by him early in

[2] This is the style of so many extended Indian narratives that I venture to call it characteristic. It has long been clear that there are important differences between the styles of oral and written narratives. (FWT)

January, 1906. He had agreed to come to my study on a certain date, but at the appointed hour the interpreter came alone, and said that Geronimo was very sick with cold and fever. He had come to tell me that we must appoint another date, as he feared the old warrior had an attack of pneumonia. It was a cold day and the interpreter drew a chair up to the grate to warm himself after the exposure of the long ride. Just as he was seating himself he looked out of the window, then rose quickly, and without speaking pointed to a rapidly moving object coming our way. In a moment I recognized the old chief riding furiously (evidently trying to arrive as soon as the interpreter did), his horse flecked with foam and reeling from exhaustion. Dismounting he came in and said in a hoarse whisper, "I promised to come. I am here."

I explained to him that I had not expected him to come on such a stormy day, and that in his physical condition he must not try to work. He stood for some time, and then without speaking left the room, remounted his tired pony, and with bowed head faced ten long miles of cold north wind—he had kept his promise.

When he had finished his story I submitted the manuscript to Major Charles W. Taylor, Eighteenth Cavalry, commandant, Fort Sill, Oklahoma, who gave me some valuable suggestions as to additional related information which I asked Geronimo to give. In most cases the old chief gave the desired information, but in some instances he refused, stating his reasons for so doing.

When the added information had been incorporated I submitted the manuscript to President Roosevelt, from whose letter I quote: "This is a very interesting volume which you have in manuscript, but I would advise that you disclaim responsibility in all cases where the reputation of an individual is assailed."

In accordance with that suggestion, I have appended notes throughout the book disclaiming responsibility for adverse criticisms of any persons mentioned by Geronimo.

On June 2d, 1906, I transmitted the complete manuscript to the War Department. The following quotation is from the letter of transmission:

"In accordance with endorsement number eight of the 'Brief' submitted to me by the commanding officer of Fort Sill, which endorsement constituted the instructions of the Department, I submit herewith manuscript of the Autobiography of Geronimo.

"The manuscript has been submitted to the President, and at his suggestion I have disclaimed any responsibility for the criticisms (made by Geronimo) of individuals mentioned."

Six weeks after the manuscript was forwarded, Thomas C. Barry, Brigadier General, Assistant to the Chief of Staff, sent to the President the following:

MEMORANDUM FOR THE SECRETARY OF WAR.
"Subject: Manuscript of the Autobiography of Geronimo. The paper herewith, which was referred to this office on July 6th, with instruc-

tions to report as to whether there is anything objectionable in it, is returned.

"The manuscript is an interesting autobiography of a notable Indian, made by himself. There are a number of passages which, from the departmental point of view, are decidedly objectionable. These are found on pages 73, 74, 90, 91, and 97, and are indicated by marginal lines in red. The entire manuscript appears in a way important as showing the Indian side of a prolonged controversy, but it is believed that the document, either in whole or in part, should not receive the approval of the War Department."

The memorandum is published that the objections of the War Department may be made known to the public.

The objection is raised to the mention on page 122 of the book of an attack upon Indians in a tent at Apache Pass or Bowie, by U.S. soldiers. The statement of Geronimo is, however, substantially confirmed by L. C. Hughes, editor of *The Star*, Tucson, Arizona.

On pages 135–6 and 139 of the book, Geronimo criticized General Crook. This criticism is simply Geronimo's private opinion of General Crook. We deem it a personal matter and leave it without comment, as it in no way concerns the history of the Apaches.

On page 143 of the book Geronimo accuses General Miles of bad faith. Of course, General Miles made the treaty with the Apaches, but we know very well that he is not responsible for the way the Government subsequently treated the prisoners of war. However, Geronimo cannot understand this and fixes upon General Miles the blame for what he calls unjust treatment.

One could not expect the Department of War to approve adverse criticisms of its own acts, but it is especially gratifying that such a liberal view has been taken of these criticisms, and also that such a frank statement of the merits of the Autobiography is submitted in the memorandum. Of course neither the President nor the War Department is in any way responsible for what Geronimo says; he has simply been granted the opportunity to state his own case as he sees it.

The fact that Geronimo has told the story in his own way is doubtless the only excuse necessary to offer for the many unconventional features of this work.

PART I
The Apaches

1

ORIGIN OF THE
APACHE INDIANS

IN the beginning the world was covered with darkness. There was no sun, no day. The perpetual night had no moon or stars.

There were, however, all manner of beasts and birds. Among the beasts were many hideous, nameless monsters, as well as dragons, lions, tigers, wolves, foxes, beavers, rabbits, squirrels, rats, mice, and all manner of creeping things such as lizards and serpents. Mankind could not prosper under such conditions, for the beasts and serpents destroyed all human offspring.

All creatures had the power of speech and were gifted with reason.

There were two tribes of creatures: the birds or the feathered tribe and the beasts. The former were organized under their chief, the eagle.

These tribes often held councils, and the birds wanted light admitted. This the beasts repeatedly refused to do. Finally the birds made war against the beasts.

The beasts were armed with clubs, but the eagle had taught his tribe to use bows and arrows. The serpents were so wise that they could not all be killed. One took refuge in a perpendicular cliff of a mountain in Arizona, and his eyes (changed into a brilliant stone) may be seen in that rock to this day. The bears, when killed, would each be changed into several other bears, so that the more bears the feathered tribe killed, the more there were. The dragon could not be killed, either, for he was covered with four coats of horny scales, and the arrows would not penetrate these. One of the most hideous, vile monsters (nameless) was proof against arrows, so the eagle flew high up in the air with a round, white stone, and let it fall on this monster's head, killing him instantly. This was such a good service that the stone was called sacred.[1] They fought for many days, but at last the birds won the victory.

After this war was over, although some evil beasts remained, the birds were able to control the councils, and light was admitted. Then mankind could live and prosper. The eagle was chief in this good fight: therefore, his feathers were worn by man as emblems of wisdom, justice, and power.

Among the few human beings that were yet alive was a woman who had been blessed with many children, but these had always been de-

---

[1] A symbol of this stone is used in the tribal game of Kah. See Chapter IV. (SMB)

stroyed by the beasts. If by any means she succeeded in eluding the others, the dragon, who was very wise and very evil, would come himself and eat her babes.

After many years a son of the rainstorm was born to her and she dug for him a deep cave.[2] The entrance to this cave she closed and over the spot built a camp fire. This concealed the babe's hiding place and kept him warm. Every day she would remove the fire and descend into the cave, where the child's bed was, to nurse him; then she would return and rebuild the camp fire.

Frequently the dragon would come and question her, but she would say, "I have no more children; you have eaten all of them."

When the child was larger he would not always stay in the cave, for he sometimes wanted to run and play. Once the dragon saw his tracks. Now this perplexed and enraged the old dragon, for he could not find the hiding place of the boy; but he said that he would destroy the mother if she did not reveal the child's hiding place. The poor mother was very much troubled; she could not give up her child, but she knew the power and cunning of the dragon, therefore she lived in constant fear.

[2] In the Chiricahua creation myth which Geronimo tells here the woman's name is White Painted Woman. The heroic child is called Child of the Water since his father was Water in the form of a rainstorm. The other principal character is Killer of Enemies, usually referred to as the child's brother rather than his uncle as here. Interestingly, Geronimo portrays Killer of Enemies as cowardly, for in another episode of this myth this character chooses the things which the whites will use in life while Child of the Water chooses those things for the Chiricahua. (FWT)

Soon after this the boy said that he wished to go hunting. The mother would not give her consent. She told him of the dragon, the wolves, and serpents; but he said, "To-morrow I go."

At the boy's request his uncle (who was the only man then living) made a little bow and some arrows for him, and the two went hunting the next day. They trailed the deer far up the mountain and finally the boy killed a buck. His uncle showed him how to dress the deer and broil the meat. They broiled two hind quarters, one for the child and one for his uncle. When the meat was done they placed it on some bushes to cool. Just then the huge form of the dragon appeared. The child was not afraid, but his uncle was so dumb with fright that he did not speak or move.

The dragon took the boy's parcel of meat and went aside with it. He placed the meat on another bush and seated himself beside it. Then he said, "This is the child I have been seeking. Boy, you are nice and fat, so when I have eaten this venison I shall eat you." The boy said, "No, you shall not eat me, and you shall not eat that meat." So he walked over to where the dragon sat and took the meat back to his own seat. The dragon said, "I like your courage, but you are foolish; what do you think you could do?" "Well," said the boy, "I can do enough to protect myself, as you may find out." Then the dragon took the meat again, and then the boy retook it. Four times in all the dragon took the meat, and after the fourth time the boy replaced the meat he said, "Dragon, will you fight me?" The dragon said, "Yes, in whatever way you like." The boy said, "I will stand one hundred paces distant from you and you may have four shots at me with your bow and arrows, provided that you will then exchange places with me and give me four shots." "Good," said the dragon. "Stand up."

Then the dragon took his bow, which was made of a large pine tree. He took four arrows from his quiver; they were made of young pine tree saplings, and each arrow was twenty feet in length. He took deliberate aim, but just as the arrow left the bow the boy made a peculiar sound and leaped into the air. Immediately the arrow was shivered into a thousand splinters, and the boy was seen standing on the top of a bright rainbow over the spot where the dragon's aim had been directed. Soon the rainbow was gone and the boy was standing on the ground again. Four times this was repeated, then the boy said, "Dragon, stand here: it is my time to shoot." The dragon said, "All right, your little arrows cannot pierce my first coat of horn, and I have three other coats —shoot away." The boy shot an arrow, striking the dragon just over the heart, and one coat of the great horny scales fell to the ground. The next shot another coat, and then another, and the dragon's heart was exposed. Then the dragon trembled, but could not move. Before the fourth arrow was shot the boy said, "Uncle, you are dumb with fear; you have not moved; come here or the dragon will fall on you." His uncle ran toward him. Then he sped the fourth arrow with true aim, and it pierced the dragon's heart. With a tremendous roar the dragon rolled down the mountain side—down four precipices into a cañon below.

Immediately storm clouds swept the mountains, lightning flashed, thunder rolled, and the rain poured. When the rainstorm had passed, far down in the cañon below, they could see fragments of the huge body of the dragon lying among the rocks, and the bones of this dragon may still be found there.

This boy's name was Apache. Usen[8] taught him how to prepare herbs for medicine, how to hunt, and how to fight. He was the first chief of the Indians and wore the eagle's feathers as the sign of justice, wisdom, and power. To him, and to his people, as they were created, Usen gave homes in the land of the West.

---

[8] "Usen" is the Apache word for God. It is used here because it implies the attributes of deity that are held in their primitive religion. "Apache" means "Enemy." (SMB)

2

SUBDIVISIONS OF THE APACHE TRIBE

THE Apache Indians are divided into six sub-tribes. To one of these, the Be-don-ko-he, I belong.[1]

Our tribe inhabited that region of mountainous country which lies west from the east line of Arizona, and south from the headwaters of the Gila River.

East of us lived the Chi-hen-ne (Ojo Caliente), (Hot Springs) Apaches. Our tribe never had any difficulty with them. Victoria, their chief, was

[1] Throughout this complicated discussion Geronimo is largely talking about the various bands and local groups of the Chiricahua Apache; one such band was sometimes (and confusingly) called the Chiracahua. A band, according to Opler (*An Apache Life-Way*) "is a division of the tribe based on territory, including within its borders those local groups near enough to unite for military action if the need arises or to cooperate for any important social occasion." The Bedonkohe whom Geronimo calls his own people appear to have been such a band. (FWT)

always a friend to me. He always helped our tribe when we asked him for help. He lost his life in the defense of the rights of his people.[2] He was a good man and a brave warrior. His son Charlie now lives here in this reservation with us.

North of us lived the White Mountain Apaches. They were not always on the best of terms with our tribe, yet we seldom had any war with them. I knew their chief, Hash-ka-ai-la, personally, and I considered him a good warrior. Their range was next to that of the Navajo Indians, who were not of the same blood as the Apaches. We held councils with all Apache tribes, but never with the Navajo Indians. However, we traded with them and sometimes visited them.

To the west of our country ranged the Chi-e-a-hen Apaches. They had two chiefs within my time, Co-si-to and Co-da-hoo-yah. They were friendly, but not intimate with our tribe.

South of us lived the Cho-kon-en (Chiricahua) Apaches, whose chief in the old days was Cochise, and later his son, Naiche. This tribe was always on the most friendly terms with us. We were often in camp and on the trail together. Naiche, who was my companion in arms, is now my companion in bondage.

[2] Killed by Mexican troops, October 14, 1880, after several months of running warfare. Faulk (*The Geronimo Campaign*) writes that one Mauricio Corredor killed Victoria (also, and more regularly, Victorio); this same individual is said to have killed Captain Emmet Crawford, January 11, 1886, while the latter was pursuing Geronimo in the Sierra Madre. (FWT)

To the south and west of us lived the Ned-ni Apaches. Their chief was Whoa, called by the Mexicans Capitan Whoa. They were our firm friends. The land of this tribe lies partly in Old Mexico and partly in Arizona.[3] Whoa and I often camped and fought side by side as brothers. My enemies were his enemies, my friends his friends. He is dead now, but his son Asa is interpreting this story for me.[4]

Still the four tribes (Bedonkohe, Chokonen, Chihenne, and Nedni), who were fast friends in the days of freedom, cling together as they decrease in number. Only the destruction of all our people would dissolve our bonds of friendship.

We are vanishing from the earth, yet I cannot think we are useless or Usen would not have created us. He created all tribes of men and certainly had a righteous purpose in creating each.

For each tribe of men Usen created He also made a home. In the land created for any particular tribe He placed whatever would be best for the welfare of that tribe.

When Usen created the Apaches He also created their homes in the West. He gave to them

[3] The boundary lines established at different times between Mexico and the United States did not conform to the boundary lines of these Apache tribes, of course, and the Indians soon saw and took advantage of the international questions arising from the conflicting interests of the two governments. (SMB)

[4] Whoa, also called Juh and Who, died in late May or early June, 1883, when returning from a peace mission at Casa Grandes. Some reports say that he was drunk when he fell from his mule into a stream and drowned, but his son Asa, who was with him at the time, says that he died of a heart attack. (FWT)

such grain, fruits, and game as they needed to eat. To restore their health when disease attacked them He made many different herbs to grow. He taught them where to find these herbs, and how to prepare them for medicine. He gave them a pleasant climate and all they needed for clothing and shelter was at hand.

Thus it was in the beginning: the Apaches and their homes each created for the other by Usen himself. When they are taken from these homes they sicken and die. How long[5] will it be until it is said, there are no Apaches?

[5] The Apache Indians held prisoners of war are greatly decreasing in numbers. There seems to be no particular cause but nevertheless their numbers grow smaller. (SMB)

3

EARLY LIFE

I was born in No-doyohn Cañon, Arizona, June, 1829.

In that country which lies around the headwaters of the Gila River I was reared. This range was our fatherland; among these mountains our wigwams were hidden; the scattered valleys contained our fields; the boundless prairies, stretching away on every side, were our pastures; the rocky caverns were our burying places.

I was fourth in a family of eight children—four boys and four girls.[1] Of that family, only myself, my brother, Porico (White Horse), and

---

[1] Geronimo is the fourth of a family of four boys and four girls. He has had four wives that were full-blood Bedonkohe Apaches, and four that were part Bedonkohe Apache and part other Apache blood. Four of his children have been killed by Mexicans and four have been held in bondage by the U.S. Government. He firmly believes in destiny and in the magic of the number four. Besides Geronimo, only four full-blood Bedonkohe Apaches are now living. They are Porico (White Horse), Nah-da-ste, Mah-ta-neal, and To-klon-nen. (SMB)

my sister, Nah-da-ste, are yet alive. We are held as prisoners of war in this Military Reservation (Fort Sill).

As a babe I rolled on the dirt floor of my father's tepee, hung in my tsoch (Apache name for cradle) at my mother's back, or suspended from the bough of a tree. I was warmed by the sun, rocked by the winds, and sheltered by the trees as other Indian babes.

When a child my mother taught me the legends of our people; taught me of the sun and sky, the moon and stars, the clouds and storms. She also taught me to kneel and pray to Usen for strength, health, wisdom, and protection. We never prayed against any person, but if we had aught against any individual we ourselves took vengeance. We were taught that Usen does not care for the petty quarrels of men.

My father had often told me of the brave deeds of our warriors, of the pleasures of the chase, and the glories of the warpath.

With my brothers and sisters I played about my father's home. Sometimes we played at hide-and-seek among the rocks and pines; sometimes we loitered in the shade of the cottonwood trees or sought the shudock (a kind of wild cherry) while our parents worked in the field. Sometimes we played that we were warriors. We would practice stealing upon some object that represented an enemy, and in our childish imitation often perform the feats of war. Sometimes we would hide away from our mother to see if she could find us, and often when thus concealed go to sleep and perhaps remain hidden for many hours.

When we were old enough to be of real service we went to the field with our parents: not to play, but to toil. When the crops were to be planted we broke the ground with wooden hoes. We planted the corn in straight rows, the beans among the corn, and the melons and pumpkins in irregular order over the field. We cultivated these crops as there was need.[2]

Our field usually contained about two acres of ground. The fields were never fenced. It was common for many families to cultivate land in the same valley and share the burden of protecting the growing crops from destruction by the ponies of the tribe, or by deer and other wild animals.

Melons were gathered as they were consumed. In the autumn pumpkins and beans were gathered and placed in bags or baskets; ears of corn were tied together by the husks, and then the harvest was carried on the backs of ponies up to our homes. Here the corn was shelled, and all the harvest stored away in caves or other secluded places to be used in winter.

We never fed corn to our ponies, but if we kept them up in the winter time we gave them fodder to eat. We had no cattle or other domestic animals except our dogs and ponies.

[2] There is considerable dispute as to the practice of agriculture among the Chiricahua in pre-white times. They were nomadic but did settle for periods of time in a particular locale. And they could easily have learned planting and harvesting from the Mexicans. (FWT)

We did not cultivate tobacco, but found it growing wild. This we cut and cured in autumn, but if the supply ran out the leaves from the stalks left standing served our purpose. All Indians smoked—men and women.[3] No boy was allowed to smoke until he had hunted alone and killed large game—wolves and bears. Unmarried women were not prohibited from smoking, but were considered immodest if they did so. Nearly all matrons smoked.

Besides grinding the corn (by hand with stone mortars and pestles) for bread, we sometimes crushed it and soaked it, and after it had fermented made from this juice a "tis-win," which had the power of intoxication, and was very highly prized by the Indians. This work was done by the squaws and children. When berries or nuts were to be gathered the small children and the squaws would go in parties to hunt them, and sometimes stay all day. When they went any great distance from camp they took ponies to carry the baskets.

I frequently went with these parties, and upon one of these excursions a woman named Cho-ko-le got lost from the party and was riding her pony through a thicket in search of her friends. Her little dog was following as she slowly made her way through the thick underbrush and pine trees. All at once a grizzly bear rose in her path and attacked the pony. She jumped off and her

---

[3] The Apaches did not smoke the peace pipe, unless it was proposed by some other Indians. They had no large pipes; in fact, they usually smoked cigarettes made by rolling the tobacco in wrappers of oak leaves. (SMB)

pony escaped, but the bear attacked her, so she fought him the best she could with her knife. Her little dog, by snapping at the bear's heels and distracting his attention from the woman, enabled her for some time to keep pretty well out of his reach. Finally the grizzly struck her over the head, tearing off almost her whole scalp. She fell, but did not lose consciousness, and while prostrate struck him four good licks with her knife, and he retreated. After he had gone she replaced her torn scalp and bound it up as best she could, then she turned deathly sick and had to lie down. That night her pony came into camp with his load of nuts and berries, but no rider. The Indians hunted for her, but did not find her until the second day. They carried her home, and under the treatment of their medicine men all her wounds were healed.

The Indians knew what herbs to use for medicine, how to prepare them, and how to give the medicine. This they had been taught by Usen in the beginning, and each succeeding generation had men who were skilled in the art of healing.

In gathering the herbs, in preparing them, and in administering the medicine, as much faith was held in prayer as in the actual effect of the medicine. Usually about eight persons worked together in making medicine, and there were forms of prayer and incantations to attend each stage of the process. Four attended to the incantations and four to the preparation of the herbs.

Some of the Indians were skilled in cutting out bullets, arrow heads, and other missiles with which warriors were wounded. I myself have done much of this, using a common dirk or butcher knife.[4]

Small children wore very little clothing in winter and none in the summer. Women usually wore a primitive skirt, which consisted of a piece of cotton cloth fastened about the waist, and extending to the knees. Men wore breach cloths and moccasins. In winter they had shirts and leggings in addition.

Frequently when the tribe was in camp a number of boys and girls, by agreement, would steal away and meet at a place several miles distant, where they could play all day free from tasks. They were never punished for these frolics; but if their hiding places were discovered they were ridiculed.

---

[4] The only foundation for the statement, frequently made, that Geronimo was a medicine man. (SMB)

But numerous other accounts suggest that Geronimo was a "medicine man" and that his powers of divination and healing made him feared and perhaps even disliked by not a few of his own people. I have called him a war shaman in my Introduction. (FWT)

4

TRIBAL AMUSEMENTS, MANNERS, AND CUSTOMS

To celebrate each noted event a feast and dance would be given. Perhaps only our own people, perhaps neighboring tribes, would be invited. These festivities usually lasted for about four days. By day we feasted, by night under the direction of some chief we danced. The music for our dance was singing led by the warriors, and accompanied by beating the esadadedne (buckskin-on-a-hoop). No words were sung—only the tones. When the feasting and dancing were over we would have horse races, foot races, wrestling, jumping, and all sorts of games (gambling).

Among these games the most noted was the tribal game of Kah (foot). It is played as follows: Four moccasins are placed about four feet apart in holes in the ground, dug in a row on one side of the camp, and on the opposite side a similar parallel row. At night a camp fire is started between these two rows of moccasins, and the players are arranged on sides, one or any number on each side. The score is kept by a bundle of sticks, from which each side takes a stick for every point won. First one side takes the bone,[1] puts up blankets between the four moccasins and the fire so that the opposing team cannot observe their movements, and then begin to sing the legends of creation. The side having the bone represents the feathered tribe, the opposite side represents the beasts. The players representing the birds do all the singing, and while singing hide the bone in one of the moccasins, then the blankets are thrown down. They continue to sing, but as soon as the blankets are thrown down the chosen player from the opposing team, armed with a war club, comes to their side of the camp fire and with his club strikes the moccasin in which he thinks the bone is hidden. If he strikes the right moccasin, his side gets the bone, and in turn represents the birds, while the opposing team must keep quiet and guess in turn. There are only four plays; three that lose and one that wins. When all the sticks are gone from the bundle the side having the largest number of sticks is counted winner.

This game is seldom played except as a gambling game, but for the purpose it is the most popular game known to the tribe. Usually the game lasts four or five hours. It is never played in daytime.

---

[1] A symbol of the white rock used by the eagle in slaying the nameless monster—see Chapter I. (SMB)

After the games are all finished the visitors say, "We are satisfied," and the camp is broken up. I was always glad when the dances and feasts were announced. So were all the other young people.

Our life also had a religious side. We had no churches, no religious organizations, no sabbath day, no holidays, and yet we worshiped. Sometimes the whole tribe would assemble to sing and pray; sometimes a smaller number, perhaps only two or three. The songs had a few words, but were not formal. The singer would occasionally put in such words as he wished instead of the usual tone sound. Sometimes we prayed in silence; sometimes each one prayed aloud; sometimes an aged person prayed for all of us. At other times one would rise and speak to us of our duties[2] to each other and to Usen. Our services were short.

When disease or pestilence abounded we were assembled and questioned by our leaders to ascertain what evil we had done, and how Usen could be satisfied. Sometimes sacrifice was deemed necessary. Sometimes the offending one was punished.

If an Apache had allowed his aged parents to suffer for food or shelter, if he had neglected or abused the sick, if he had profaned our religion,

[2] The Apaches recognized no duties to any man outside their tribe. It was no sin to kill enemies or to rob them. However, if they accepted any favor from a stranger, or allowed him to share their comforts in any way, he became (by adoption) related to the tribe and they must recognize their duty to him. (SMB)

or had been unfaithful, he might be banished from the tribe.

The Apaches had no prisons as white men have. Instead of sending their criminals into prison they sent them out of their tribe. These faithless, cruel, lazy, or cowardly members of the tribe were excluded in such a manner that they could not join any other tribe. Neither could they have any protection from our unwritten tribal laws. Frequently these outlaw Indians banded together and committed depredations which were charged against the regular tribe. However, the life of an outlaw Indian was a hard lot, and their bands never became very large; besides, these bands frequently provoked the wrath of the tribe and secured their own destruction.

When I was about eight or ten years old I began to follow the chase, and to me this was never work.

Out on the prairies, which ran up to our mountain homes, wandered herds of deer, antelope, elk, and buffalo, to be slaughtered when we needed them.

Usually we hunted buffalo on horseback, killing them with arrows and spears. Their skins were used to make tepees and bedding; their flesh, to eat.

It required more skill to hunt the deer than any other animal. We never tried to approach a deer except against the wind. Frequently we would spend hours in stealing upon grazing deer. If they were in the open we would crawl long distances on the ground, keeping a weed or brush before us, so that our approach would not be noticed. Often we could kill several out of one herd before the others would run away. Their flesh was dried and packed in vessels, and would keep in this condition for many months. The hide of the deer was soaked in water and ashes and the hair removed, and then the process of tanning continued until the buckskin was soft and pliable. Perhaps no other animal was more valuable to us than the deer.

In the forests and along the streams were many wild turkeys. These we would drive to the plains, then slowly ride up toward them until they were almost tired out. When they began to drop and hide we would ride in upon them and, by swinging from the side of our horses, catch them. If one started to fly we would ride swiftly under him and kill him with a short stick, or hunting club. In this way we could usually get as many wild turkeys as we could carry home on a horse.

There were many rabbits in our range, and we also hunted them on horseback. Our horses were trained to follow the rabbit at full speed, and as they approached them we would swing from one side of the horse and strike the rabbit with our hunting club. If he was too far away we would throw the stick and kill him. This was great sport when we were boys, but as warriors we seldom hunted small game.

There were many fish in the streams, but as we did not eat them, we did not try to catch or kill them. Small boys sometimes threw stones at them or shot at them for practice with their bows and arrows. Usen did not intend snakes, frogs, or fishes to be eaten. I have never eaten of them.[3]

There were many eagles in the mountains. These we hunted for their feathers. It required great skill to steal upon an eagle, for besides having sharp eyes, he is wise and never stops at any place where he does not have a good view of the surrounding country.

I have killed many bears with a spear, but was never injured in a fight with one. I have killed several mountain lions with arrows, and one with a spear. Both bears and mountain lions are good for food and valuable for their skin. When we killed them we carried them home on our horses. We often made quivers for our arrows from the skin of the mountain lion. These were very pretty and very durable.

During my minority we had never seen a missionary or a priest. We had never seen a white man. Thus quietly lived the Be-don-ko-he Apaches.

---

[3] This is not idiosyncratic on Geronimo's part, but a cultural taboo. Reptiles were not acceptable food nor were other creatures which were believed to eat them. (FWT)

5

THE FAMILY

My grandfather, Maco, had been our chief. I never saw him, but my father often told me of the great size, strength, and sagacity of this old warrior. Their principal wars had been with the Mexicans. They had some wars with other tribes of Indians also, but were seldom at peace for any great length of time with the Mexican towns.

Maco died when my father was but a young warrior, and Mangus-Colorado[1] became chief of the Bedonkohe Apaches. When I was but a small boy my father died, after having been sick for some time. When he passed away, carefully the watchers closed his eyes, then they arrayed him in his best clothes, painted his face afresh,

[1] Maco was chief of the Nedni Apaches. His son (Geronimo's father) had married a Bedonkohe Apache (Geronimo's mother) and joined her tribe, thereby losing his right to rule by heredity. By this it will be seen Geronimo could not become chief by hereditary right, although his grandfather was a chieftain. It is also shown that Geronimo's father could not be chief, hence the accession of Mangus-Colorado. (SMB)

wrapped a rich blanket around him, saddled his
favorite horse, bore his arms in front of him, and
led his horse behind, repeating in wailing tones
his deeds of valor as they carried his body to a
cave in the mountain. Then they slew his horses,
and we gave away all of his other property, as
was customary in our tribe, after which his body
was deposited in the cave, his arms beside him.[2]
His grave is hidden by piles of stone. Wrapped
in splendor he lies in seclusion, and the winds in
the pines sing a low requiem over the dead warrior.

After my father's death I assumed the care of
my mother. She never married again, although
according to the customs of our tribe she might
have done so immediately after his death. Usually, however, the widow who has children remains single after her husband's death for two
or three years; but the widow without children
marries again immediately. After a warrior's
death his widow returns to her people and may
be given away or sold by her father or brothers.
My mother chose to live with me, and she never
desired to marry again. We lived near our old
home and I supported her.

In 1846, being seventeen years of age, I was
admitted to the council of the warriors. Then I

[2] The Apaches will not keep any of the property of a
deceased relative. Their unwritten tribal laws forbid it, because they think that otherwise the children or other relatives of one who had much property might be glad when
their father or relatives died. (SBM)

It should also be noted that such practices manifest the
profound Chiricahua fear of ghosts. (FWT)

was very happy, for I could go wherever I wanted and do whatever I liked. I had not been under the control of any individual, but the customs of our tribe prohibited me from sharing the glories of the warpath until the council admitted me. When opportunity offered, after this, I could go on the warpath with my tribe. This would be glorious. I hoped soon to serve my people in battle. I had long desired to fight with our warriors.

Perhaps the greatest joy to me was that now I could marry the fair Alope, daughter of No-po-so. She was a slender, delicate girl, but we had been lovers for a long time. So, as soon as the council granted me these privileges I went to see her father concerning our marriage. Perhaps our love was of no interest to him; perhaps he wanted to keep Alope with him, for she was a dutiful daughter; at any rate he asked many ponies for her. I made no reply, but in a few days appeared before his wigwam with the herd of ponies and took with me Alope. This was all the marriage ceremony necessary in our tribe.

Not far from my mother's tepee I had made for us a new home. The tepee was made of buffalo hides and in it were many bear robes, lion hides, and other trophies of the chase, as well as my spears, bows, and arrows. Alope had made many little decorations of beads and drawn work on buckskin, which she placed in our tepee.[3] She

---

[3] Beads were obtained from the Mexicans. The Apaches also got money from the Mexicans, but deemed it of no value, and either gave it to their children to play with or threw it away. (SBM)

also drew many pictures on the walls of our home. She was a good wife, but she was never strong. We followed the traditions of our fathers and were happy. Three children came to us—children that played, loitered, and worked as I had done.

PART II
The Mexicans

6

KAS-KI-YEH

PART I—THE MASSACRE

In the summer of 1858, being at peace with the Mexican towns as well as with all the neighboring Indian tribes, we went south into Old Mexico to trade.[1] Our whole tribe (Bedonkohe Apaches) went through Sonora toward Casa Grande, our destination, but just before reaching that place we stopped at another Mexican town called by the Indians "Kas-ki-yeh." Here we stayed for several days, camping outside the city. Every day we would go into town to trade, leaving our camp under the protection of a small guard so that our

[1] Most of these dates should be taken as approximations, but this should not lead the reader (as it has led many) to assume that *all* details are highly fictionalized because the Chiricahua kept no written records. A nonliterate people of necessity develops habits of mind which give rise to incredible feats of memory such as those mentioned in so many of the early missionary accounts of American Indians. The whole history and customs of a tribe exist only in memory, and this is therefore a highly-prized mental attribute. (FWT)

arms, supplies, and women and children would not be disturbed during our absence.

Late one afternoon when returning from town we were met by a few women and children who told us that Mexican troops from some other town had attacked our camp, killed all the warriors of the guard, captured all our ponies, secured our arms, destroyed our supplies, and killed many of our women and children.[2] Quickly we separated, concealing ourselves as best we could until nightfall, when we assembled at our appointed place of rendezvous—a thicket by the river. Silently we stole in one by one: sentinels were placed, and, when all were counted, I found that my aged mother, my young wife, and my three small children were among the slain. There were no lights in camp, so without being noticed I silently turned away and stood by the river. How long I stood there I do not know, but when I saw the warriors arranging for a council I took my place.

That night I did not give my vote for or against any measure; but it was decided that as there were only eighty warriors left, and as we were without arms or supplies, and were furthermore surrounded by the Mexicans far inside their own territory, we could not hope to fight success-

[2] Such an incident was typical of Chiricahua/Mexican relations: when one party acted in peace the other acted in treachery. Here we have illustrated the classic Mexican ploy of trading while preparing a surprise attack. Often the male Chiricahua were beguiled by drink and then either executed or enslaved for use in northern Mexico or on the chicle plantations of Yucatán. (FWT)

fully So our chief, Mangus-Colorado, gave the order to start at once in perfect silence for our homes in Arizona, leaving the dead upon the field.

I stood until all had passed, hardly knowing what I would do—I had no weapon, nor did I hardly wish to fight, neither did I contemplate recovering the bodies of my loved ones, for that was forbidden. I did not pray, nor did I resolve to do anything in particular, for I had no purpose left. I finally followed the tribe silently, keeping just within hearing distance of the soft noise of the feet of the retreating Apaches.

The next morning some of the Indians killed a small amount of game and we halted long enough for the tribe to cook and eat, when the march was resumed. I had killed no game, and did not eat. During the first march as well as while we were camped at this place I spoke to no one and no one spoke to me—there was nothing to say.[3]

For two days and three nights we were on forced marches, stopping only for meals, then we made a camp near the Mexican border, where we rested two days. Here I took some food and talked with the other Indians who had lost in the massacre, but none had lost as I had, for I had lost all.

Within a few days we arrived at our own settlement. There were the decorations that Alope had made—and there were the playthings of our

---

[3] The Chiricahua considered emotional demonstrations unbecoming since anything deeply felt could be translated into actions. (FWT)

little ones. I burned them all, even our tepee.[4] I also burned my mother's tepee and destroyed all her property.

I was never again contented in our quiet home. True, I could visit my father's grave, but I had vowed vengeance upon the Mexican troopers who had wronged me, and whenever I came near his grave or saw anything to remind me of former happy days my heart would ache for revenge upon Mexico.

PART II—REVENGE

As soon as we had again collected some arms and supplies Mangus-Colorado, our chief, called a council and found that all our warriors were willing to take the warpath against Mexico. I was appointed to solicit the aid of other tribes in this war.

When I went to the Chokonen (Chiricahua) Apaches, Cochise, their chief, called a council at early dawn. Silently the warriors assembled at an open place in a mountain dell and took their seats on the ground, arranged in rows according to their ranks. Silently they sat smoking. At a signal from the chief I arose and presented my cause as follows:

"Kinsman, you have heard what the Mexicans have recently done without cause. You are my relatives—uncles, cousins, brothers. We are men the same as the Mexicans are—we can do to them

[4] According to custom he should not have kept the property of his deceased relatives, but he was not compelled to destroy his own tepee or the playthings of his children. (SMB)

what they have done to us. Let us go forward
and trail them—I will lead you to their city—
we will attack them in their homes. I will fight in
the front of the battle—I only ask you to follow
me to avenge this wrong done by these Mexicans
—will you come? It is well—you will all come.

"Remember the rule in war—men may return
or they may be killed. If any of these young men
are killed I want no blame from their kinsmen,
for they themselves have chosen to go. If I am
killed no one need mourn for me. My people have
all been killed in that country, and I, too, will die
if need be."

I returned to my own settlement, reported this
success to my chieftain, and immediately de-
parted to the southward into the land of the Nedni Apaches. Their chief, Whoa, heard me without comment, but he immediately issued orders
for a council, and when all were ready gave a sign
that I might speak. I addressed them as I had addressed the Chokonen tribe, and they also promised to help us.

It was in the summer of 1859, almost a year
from the date of the massacre of Kaskiyeh, that
these three tribes were assembled on the Mexican
border to go upon the warpath. Their faces were
painted, the war bands[5] fastened upon their
brows their long scalp-locks[6] ready for the hand

---

[5] Strips of buckskin about two inches wide fastened
around the head. (SMB)

[6] At this time the Mexican Government offered a reward
in gold for Apache scalps—one hundred dollars for warrior's
scalp, fifty dollars for squaw's scalp, and twenty-five dollars
for child's scalp. (SMB)

and knife of the warrior who would overcome them. Their families had been hidden away in a mountain rendezvous near the Mexican border. With these families a guard was posted, and a number of places of rendezvous designated in case the camp should be disturbed.

When all were ready the chieftains gave command to go forward. None of us were mounted and each warrior wore moccasins and also a cloth wrapped about his loins. This cloth could be spread over him when he slept, and when on the march would be ample protection as clothing. In battle, if the fight was hard, we did not wish much clothing. Each warrior carried three days' rations, but as we often killed game while on the march, we seldom were without food.

We traveled in three divisions: the Bedonkohe Apaches led by Mangus-Colorado, the Chokonen Apaches by Cochise, and the Nedni Apaches by Whoa; however, there was no regular order inside the separate tribes. We usually marched about fourteen hours per day, making three stops for meals, and traveling forty to forty-five miles a day.

I acted as guide into Mexico, and we followed the river courses and mountain ranges because we could better thereby keep our movements concealed. We entered Sonora and went southward past Quitaro, Nacozari, and many smaller settlements.

When we were almost at Arispe we camped, and eight men rode out from the city to parley with us. These we captured, killed, and scalped.

This was to draw the troops from the city, and the next day they came. The skirmishing lasted all day without a general engagement, but just at night we captured their supply train, so we had plenty of provisions and some more guns.

That night we posted sentinels and did not move our camp, but rested quietly all night, for we expected heavy work the next day. Early the next morning the warriors were assembled to pray—not for help, but that they might have health and avoid ambush or deceptions by the enemy.

As we had anticipated, about ten o'clock in the morning the whole Mexican force came out. There were two companies of cavalry and two of infantry. I recognized the cavalry as the soldiers who had killed my people at Kaskiyeh. This I told to the chieftains, and they said that I might direct the battle.

I was no chief and never had been, but because I had been more deeply wronged than others, this honor was conferred upon me, and I resolved to prove worthy of the trust. I arranged the Indians in a hollow circle near the river, and the Mexicans drew their infantry up in two lines, with the cavalry in reserve. We were in the timber, and they advanced until within about four hundred yards, when they halted and opened fire. Soon I led a charge against them, at the same time sending some braves to attack the rear. In all the battle I thought of my murdered mother, wife, and babies—of my father's grave and my vow of vengeance, and I fought with fury. Many fell by my hand, and constantly I led the advance. Many braves were killed. The battle lasted about two hours.

At the last four Indians were alone in the center of the field—myself and three other warriors. Our arrows were all gone, our spears broken off in the bodies of dead enemies. We had only our hands and knives with which to fight, but all who had stood against us were dead. Then two armed soldiers came upon us from another part of the field. They shot down two of our men and we, the remaining two, fled toward our own warriors. My companion was struck down by a saber, but I reached our warriors, seized a spear, and turned. The one who pursued me missed his aim and fell by my spear. With his saber I met the trooper who had killed my companion and we grappled and fell. I killed him with my knife and quickly rose over his body, brandishing his saber, seeking for other troopers to kill. There were none. But the Apaches had seen.[7] Over the bloody field, covered with the bodies of Mexicans, rang the fierce Apache war-whoop.

Still covered with the blood of my enemies, still holding my conquering weapon, still hot with the joy of battle, victory, and vengeance, I was surrounded by the Apache braves and made war

[7] It was by such feats of battle that Geronimo rose to leadership. Such individual exploits became part of a man's "record" within the tribe, and he was careful to confine himself to fact in his periodic recital of them; otherwise he might be contradicted and ridiculed by other witnesses. (FWT)

chief of all the Apaches. Then I gave orders for scalping the slain.[8]

I could not call back my loved ones, I could not bring back the dead Apaches, but I could rejoice in this revenge. The Apaches had avenged the massacre of "Kas-ki-yeh."

[8] From the moment the command for war is given with the Apaches everything assumes a religious guise. The manner of camping, cooking, etc., are exactly prescribed. Every object appertaining to war is called by its sacred name; as if, for instance, in English, one should say not horse, but warhorse or charger; not arrow, but missile of death. The Indian is not called by his ordinary name, but by a sacred name to which is subjoined "brave" or "chief" as the case may be. Geronimo's Indian name was Go khlä yeh, but the Mexicans at this battle called him Geronimo, a name he has borne ever since both among the Indians and white men. (SMB)

Such specialization within the culture (a vocabulary of almost one hundred war-related terms has been collected) tells us much about the old Chiricahua way and its major emphasis. (FWT)

7

FIGHTING UNDER DIFFICULTIES

ALL the other Apaches were satisfied after the battle of "Kaskiyeh," but I still desired more revenge. For several months we were busy with the chase and other peaceful pursuits. Finally I succeeded in pursuading two other warriors, Ahkoch-ne and Ko-deh-ne, to go with me to invade the Mexican country.

We left our families with the tribe and went on the warpath.[1] We were on foot and carried three days' rations. We entered Mexico on the north line of Sonora and followed the Sierra de

[1] Geronimo had married again. (SMB)

Years later a Chiricahua who apparently had read Geronimo's autobiography used this detail to "prove" that it was really Barrett who wrote the book since no Chiricahua would have remarried so soon after the death of his wife unless he married a relative or sister of hers—which Geronimo did not. But no mention is made here of how much time elapsed between the death of the first wife and the marriage to the second. (FWT)

ronimo (1829-1909). From a photograph by A. Frank
dall, 1886. *(Courtesy of the Arizona Pioneers' Historical
iety, Tucson)*

ow the Book Was Made." From the left, S. M. Barrett,
ronimo, and interpreter Asa Daklugie, second cousin of
ronimo. *(Photograph from the original edition)*

Naiche (Natchez), youngest son of Cochise and last heredita
chief of the Chiricahua Apaches. From a photograph by B
Wittick. *(Courtesy of the Bureau of American Ethnolog*
Smithsonian Institution)

Geronimo and Naiche mounted. From a photograph by C. S. Fly.
(Courtesy of the National Archives)

Hostile Chiricahuas in 1886, with Geronimo standing at center.
(From a photograph courtesy of George S. Schaeffer)

Surrender conference in the Cañon de los Embudos, Sonora, March, 1886, with Geronimo *(left, center)* and General Crook *(front, second from the right)*. From a photograph by C. S. Fly. *(Courtesy of the Arizona Pioneers' Historical Society, Tucson)*

Geronimo as a prisoner-at-work at Fort Sill. At the left is his sixth wife, Zi-yeh.

Geronimo at the wheel, a "publicity" photograph.
(Courtesy of the National Archives)

"The Last of the Bedonkhoe Apache Tribe." From the left,
Toclanny (actually a Mimbreno Apache and U.S. Army scout),
Nahdos-te (sister of Geronimo), Nah-thle-tla (first cousin of
Geronimo), and Perico (Porico) or White Horse (second
cousin of Geronimo and one of his greatest "lieutenants").
Photograph from the original edition)

The burial of Geronimo at Fort Sill, February 17, 1909.
(Courtesy of the U.S. Army Museum, Fort Sill, Oklahoma)

Geronimo. From a photograph by DeLancey Gill, 1905. *(Courtesy of the Bureau of American Ethnology, Smithsonian Institution)*

Antunez Mountains to the south end of the range. Here we decided to attack a small village. (I do not know the name of this village.) At daylight we approached from the mountains. Five horses were hitched outside. We advanced cautiously, but just before we reached the horses the Mexicans opened fire from the houses. My two companions were killed. Mexicans swarmed on every side; some were mounted; some were on foot, and all seemed to be armed. Three times that day I was surrounded, but I kept fighting, dodging, and hiding. Several times during the day while in concealment I had a chance to take deliberate aim at some Mexican, who, gun in hand, was looking for me. I do not think I missed my aim either time. With the gathering darkness I found more time to retreat toward Arizona. But the Mexicans did not quit the chase. Several times the next day mounted Mexicans tried to head me off; many times they fired on me, but I had no more arrows; so I depended upon running and hiding, although I was very tired. I had not eaten since the chase began, nor had I dared to stop for rest. The second night I got clear of my pursuers, but I never slackened my pace until I reached our home in Arizona. I came into our camp without booty, without my companions, exhausted, but not discouraged.

The wives and children of my two dead companions were cared for by their people. Some of the Apaches blamed me for the evil result of the expedition, but I said nothing. Having failed, it was only proper that I should remain silent. But

my feelings toward the Mexicans did not change
—I still hated them and longed for revenge. I
never ceased to plan for their punishment, but it
was hard to get the other warriors to listen to
my proposed raids.

In a few months after this last adventure I per-
suaded two other warriors to join me in raiding
the Mexican frontier. On our former raid we had
gone through the Nedni Apaches' range into
Sonora. This time we went through the country
of the Cho-kon-en and entered the Sierra Madre
Mountains. We traveled south, secured more rations, and prepared to begin our raids. We had
selected a village near the mountains which we
intended to attack at daylight. While asleep that
night Mexican scouts discovered our camp and
fired on us, killing one warrior. In the morning
we observed a company of Mexican troops coming from the south. They were mounted and
carried supplies for a long journey. We followed
their trail until we were sure that they were headed for our range in Arizona; then we hurried past
them and in three days reached our own settlement. We arrived at noon, and that afternoon,
about three o'clock, these Mexican troops attacked our settlement. Their first volley killed
three small boys. Many of the warriors of our
tribe were away from home, but the few of us
who were in camp were able to drive the troops
out of the mountains before night. We killed
eight Mexicans and lost five—two warriors and
three boys. The Mexicans rode due south in full
retreat. Four warriors were detailed to follow

them, and in three days these trailers returned, saying that the Mexican cavalry had left Arizona, going southward. We were quite sure they would not return soon.

Soon after this (in the summer of 1860) I was again able to take the warpath against the Mexicans, this time with twenty-five warriors. We followed the trail of the Mexican troops last mentioned and entered the Sierra de Sahuaripa Mountains. The second day in these mountains our scouts discovered mounted Mexican troops. There was only one company of cavalry in this command, and I thought that by properly surprising them we could defeat them. We ambushed the trail over which they were to come. This was at a place where the whole company must pass through a mountain defile. We reserved fire until all of the troops had passed through; then the signal was given. The Mexican troopers, seemingly without a word of command, dismounted, and placing their horses on the outside of the company, for breastworks, made a good fight against us. I saw that we could not dislodge them without using all our ammunition, so I led a charge. The warriors suddenly pressed in from all sides and we fought hand to hand. During this encounter I raised my spear to kill a Mexican soldier just as he leveled his gun at me; I was advancing rapidly, and my foot slipping in a pool of blood, I fell under the Mexican trooper. He struck me over the head with the butt of his gun, knocking me senseless. Just at that instant a warrior who followed in my footsteps killed the

Mexican with a spear. In a few minutes not a Mexican soldier was left alive. When the Apache war-cry had died away, and their enemies had been scalped, they began to care for their dead and wounded. I was found lying unconscious where I had fallen. They bathed my head in cold water and restored me to consciousness. Then they bound up my wound and the next morning, although weak from loss of blood and suffering from a severe headache, I was able to march on the return to Arizona. I did not fully recover for months, and I still wear the scar given me by that musketeer. In this fight we had lost so heavily that there really was no glory in our victory, and we returned to Arizona. No one seemed to want to go on the warpath again that year.

In the summer (1861) with twelve warriors I again went into Mexico. We entered Chihuahua and followed south on the east side of the Sierra Madre Mountains four days' journey; then crossed over to the Sierra de Sahuaripa range, not far east of Casa Grande. Here we rested one day, and sent out scouts to reconnoiter. They reported pack trains camped five miles west of us. The next morning just at daybreak, as these drivers were starting with their mule pack train, we attacked them. They rode away for their lives, leaving us the booty. The mules were loaded with provisions, most of which we took home. Two mules were loaded with side-meat or bacon; this we threw away.[2] We started to take these

---

[2] They had never eaten bacon and did not learn to do so for a long time. Even now they will not eat bacon or pork

pack trains home, going northward through Sonora, but when near Casita, Mexican troops overtook us. It was at daybreak and we were just finishing our breakfast. We had no idea that we had been pursued or that our enemies were near until they opened fire. At the first volley a bullet struck me a glancing lick just at the lower corner of the left eye and I fell unconscious. All the other Indians fled to cover. The Mexicans, thinking me dead, started in pursuit of the fleeing Indians. In a few moments I regained consciousness and had started at full speed for the woods when another company coming up opened fire on me. Then the soldiers who had been chasing the other Indians turned, and I stood between two hostile companies, but I did not stand long. Bullets whistled in every direction and at close range to me. One inflicted a slight flesh wound on my side, but I kept running, dodging, and fighting, until I got clear of my pursuers. I climbed up a steep cañon, where the cavalry could not follow. The troopers saw me, but did not dismount and try to follow. I think they were wise not to come on.

It had been understood that in case of surprise with this booty, our place of rendezvous should be the Santa Bita Mountains in Arizona. We did not reassemble in Mexico, but traveled separately and in three days we were encamped in our place of rendezvous. From this place we returned home

---

if they can get other meat. Geronimo positively refuses to eat bacon or pork. ((SMB)

This is because the Chiricahua believed that the wild hogs they knew (peccary) ate reptiles; thus all hogs did so and were taboo. (FWT)

empty-handed. We had not even a partial victory to report. I again returned wounded, but I was not yet discouraged. Again I was blamed by our people, and again I had no reply.

After our return many of the warriors had gone on a hunt and some of them had gone north to trade for blankets from the Navajo Indians. I remained at home trying to get my wounds healed. One morning just at daybreak, when the squaws were lighting the camp fires to prepare breakfast, three companies of Mexican troops who had surrounded our settlement in the night opened fire. There was no time for fighting. Men, women and children fled for their lives. Many women and children and a few warriors were killed, and four women were captured. My left eye was still swollen shut, but with the other I saw well enough to hit one of the officers with an arrow, and then make good my escape among the rocks. The troopers burned our tepees and took our arms, provisions, ponies, and blankets. Winter was at hand.

There were not more than twenty warriors in camp at this time, and only a few of us had secured weapons during the excitement of the attack. A few warriors followed the trail of the troops as they went back to Mexico with their booty, but were unable to offer battle. It was a long, long time before we were again able to go on the warpath against the Mexicans.

The four women who were captured at this time by the Mexicans were taken into Sonora, Mexico, where they were compelled to work for the Mexicans. After some years they escaped to the mountains and started to find our tribe. They had knives which they had stolen from the Mexicans, but they had no other weapons. They had no blankets; so at night they would make a little tepee by cutting brush with their knives, and setting them up for the walls. The top was covered over with brush. In this temporary tepee they would all sleep. One night when their camp fire was low they heard growling just outside the tepee. Francisco, the youngest woman of the party (about seventeen years of age), started to build up the fire, when a mountain lion crashed through the tepee and attacked her. The suddenness of the attack made her drop her knife, but she fought as best she could with her hand. She was no match for the lion, however; her left shoulder was crushed and partly torn away. The lion kept trying to catch her by the throat; this she prevented with her hands for a long time. He dragged her for about 300 yards, then she found her strength was failing her from loss of blood, and she called to the other women for help. The lion had been dragging her by one foot, and she had been catching hold of his legs, and of the rocks and underbrush, to delay him. Finally he stopped and stood over her. She again called her companions and they attacked him with their knives and killed him. Then they dressed her wounds and nursed her in the mountains for about a month. When she was again able to walk they resumed their journey and reached our tribe in safety.

This woman (Francisco) was held as a pris-

oner of war with the other Apaches and died on
the Fort Sill Reservation in 1892. Her face was
always disfigured with those scars and she never
regained perfect use of her hands. The three
older women died before we became prisoners of
war.

Many women and children were carried away
at different times by Mexicans. Not many of
them ever returned, and those who did under-
went many hardships in order to be again united
with their people. Those who did not escape were
slaves to the Mexicans, or perhaps even more de-
graded.

When warriors were captured by the Mexicans they were kept in chains. Four warriors who
were captured once at a place north of Casa
Grande, called by the Indians "Honas," were
kept in chains for a year and a half, when they
were exchanged for Mexicans whom we had
captured.

We never chained prisoners or kept them in
confinement, but they seldom got away. Mexican
men when captured were compelled to cut wood
and herd horses. Mexican women and children
were treated as our own people.[8]

[8] The interpreter Asa, son of Whoa, remembers a little
captive Mexican girl who used to play with the Apache children, but was finally exchanged.

One of Geronimo's wives and her child were killed at this
time, and thenceforth until he became a prisoner of war he
had two wives. He might have had as many wives as he
wished, but he says that he was so busy fighting Mexicans
that he could not support more than two. (SMB)

8

RAIDS THAT WERE SUCCESSFUL

In the summer of 1862 I took eight men and invaded Mexican territory. We went south on the west side of the Sierra Madre Mountains for five days; then in the night crossed over to the southern part of the Sierra de Sahuaripa range. Here we again camped to watch for pack trains. About ten o'clock next morning four drivers, mounted, came past our camp with a pack-mule train. As soon as they saw us they rode for their lives, leaving us the booty. This was a long train, and packed with blankets, calico, saddles, tinware, and loaf sugar. We hurried home as fast as we could with these provisions, and on our return while passing through a cañon in the Santa Catalina range of mountains in Arizona, met a white man driving a mule pack train. When we first saw him he had already seen us, and was riding at full tilt up the cañon. We examined his train and found that his mules were all loaded with cheese. We put them in with the other train and resumed our journey. We did not attempt to trail the driver and I am sure he did not try to follow us.

In two days we arrived at home. Then Mangus-Colorado, our chief, assembled the tribe. We gave a feast, divided the spoils, and danced all night. Some of the pack mules were killed and eaten.

This time after our return we kept out scouts so that we would know if Mexican troops should attempt to follow us.

On the third day our scouts came into camp and reported Mexican cavalry dismounted and approaching our settlement. All our warriors were in camp. Mangus-Colorado took command of one division and I of the other. We hoped to get possession of their horses, then surround the troops in the mountains, and destroy the whole company. This we were unable to do, for they too, had scouts. However, within four hours after we started we had killed ten troopers with the loss of only one man, and the Mexican cavalry was in full retreat, followed by thirty armed Apaches, who gave them no rest until they were far inside the Mexican country. No more troops came that winter.

For a long time we had plenty of provisions, plenty of blankets, and plenty of clothing. We also had plenty of cheese and sugar.

Another summer (1863) I selected three warriors and went on a raid into Mexico. We went south into Sonora, camping in the Sierra de Sahuaripa Mountains. About forty miles west of Casa Grande is a small village in the mountains, called by the Indians "Crassanas." We camped near this place and concluded to make an attack. We had noticed that just at midday no one seemed to be stirring; so we planned to make our attack at the noon hour. The next day we stole into the town at noon. We had no guns, but were armed with spears and bows and arrows. When the war-whoop was given to open the attack the Mexicans fled in every direction; not one of them made any attempt to fight us.

We shot some arrows at the retreating Mexicans, but killed only one. Soon all was silent in the town and no Mexicans could be seen.

When we discovered that all the Mexicans were gone we looked through their houses and saw many curious things. These Mexicans kept many more kinds of property than the Apaches did. Many of the things we saw in the houses we could not understand, but in the stores we saw much that we wanted; so we drove in a herd of horses and mules, and packed as much provisions and supplies as we could on them. Then we formed these animals into a pack train and returned safely to Arizona. The Mexicans did not even trail us.

When we arrived in camp we called the tribe together and feasted all day. We gave presents to everyone. That night the dance began, and it did not cease until noon the next day.

This was perhaps the most successful raid ever

made by us into Mexican territory. I do not know
the value of the booty, but it was very great, for
we had supplies enough to last our whole tribe
for a year or more.

In the fall of 1864 twenty warriors were willing to go with me on another raid into Mexico.
There were all chosen men, well armed and
equipped for battle. As usual we provided for the
safety of our families before starting on this raid.
Our whole tribe scattered and then reassembled
at a camp about forty miles from the former
place. In this way it would be hard for the Mexicans to trail them and we would know where to
find our families when we returned. Moreover,
if any hostile Indians should see this large number of warriors leaving our range they might attack our camp, but if they found no one at the
usual place their raid would fail.

We went south through the Chokonen
Apaches' range, entered Sonora, Mexico, at a
point directly south of Tombstone, Arizona, and
went into hiding in the Sierra de Antunez Mountains.

We attacked several settlements in the neigh-
borhood and secured plenty of provisions and
supplies. After about three days we attacked and
captured a mule pack train at a place called by
the Indians "Pontoco." It is situated in the mountains due west, about one day's journey from
Arispe.

There were three drivers with this train. One
was killed and two escaped. The train was loaded
with mescal, which was contained in bottles held

in wicker baskets.[1] As soon as we made camp the Indians began to get drunk and fight each other. I, too, drank enough mescal to feel the effect of it, but I was not drunk.[2] I ordered the fighting stopped, but the order was disobeyed. Soon almost a general fight was in progress. I tried to place a guard out around the camp, but all were drunk and refused to serve. I expected an attack from Mexican troops at any moment, and really it was a serious matter to me, for being in command I would be held responsible for any ill luck attending the expedition. Finally the camp became comparatively still, for the Indians were too drunk to walk or even to fight. While they were in this stupor I poured out all the mescal, then I put out all the fires and moved the pack mules to a considerable distance from camp. After this I returned to camp to try to do something for the wounded. I found that only two were dangerously wounded. From the leg of one of these I cut an arrow head, and from the shoulder of another I withdrew a spear point. When all the wounds had been cared for, I myself kept guard till morning. The next day we loaded our wounded on the pack mules and started for Arizona.

The next day we captured some cattle from a herd and drove them home with us. But it was a very difficult matter to drive cattle when we were on foot. Caring for the wounded and keeping the

---

[1] Mescal is a fiery liquor produced in Mexico from several spices of Agave. (SMB)

[2] Most sources agree that Geronimo liked his liquor as well as any of his tribesmen. (FWT)

cattle from escaping made our journey tedious. But we were not trailed, and arrived safely at home with all the booty.

We then gave a feast and dance, and divided the spoils. After the dance we killed all the cattle and dried the meat. We dressed the hides and then the dried meat was packed in between these hides and stored away. All that winter we had plenty of meat. These were the first cattle we ever had. As usual we killed and ate some of the mules. We had little use for mules, and if we could not trade them for something of value, we killed them.

In the summer of 1865, with four warriors, I went again into Mexico. Heretofore we had gone on foot; we were accustomed to fight on foot; besides, we could more easily conceal ourselves when dismounted. But this time we wanted more cattle, and it was hard to drive them when we were on foot. We entered Sonora at a point southwest from Tombstone, Arizona, and followed the Sierra de Antunez Mountains to the southern limit, then crossed the country as far south as the mouth of Yaqui River. Here we saw a great lake extending beyond the limit of sight.[3] Then we turned north, attacked several settlements, and secured plenty of supplies. When we had come back northwest of Arispe we secured about sixty head of cattle, and drove them to our homes in Arizona. We did not go directly home, but camped in different valleys with our cattle. We were not trailed. When we arrived at our

[3] Gulf of California. (SMB)

camp the tribe was again assembled for feasting and dancing. Presents were given to everybody; then the cattle were killed and the meat dried and packed.

9

VARYING FORTUNES

In the fall of 1865 with nine other warriors I went into Mexico on foot. We attacked several settlements south of Casa Grande, and collected many horses and mules. We made our way northward with these animals through the mountains. When near Arispe we made camp one evening, and thinking that we were not being trailed, turned loose the whole herd, even those we had been riding. They were in a valley surrounded by steep mountains, and we were camped at the mouth of this valley so that the animals could not leave without coming through our camp. Just as we had begun to eat our supper our scouts came in and announced Mexican troops coming toward our camp. We started for the horses, but troops that our scouts had not seen were on the cliffs above us, and opened fire. We scattered in all directions, and the troops recovered all our booty. In three days we reassembled at our appointed place of rendezvous in the Sierra Madre

Mountains in northern Sonora. Mexican troops did not follow us, and we returned to Arizona without any more fighting and with no booty. Again I had nothing to say, but I was anxious for another raid.

Early the next summer (1866) I took thirty mounted warriors and invaded Mexican territory. We went south through Chihuahua as far as Santa Cruz, Sonora, then crossed over the Sierra Madre Mountains, following the river course at the south end of the range. We kept on westward from the Sierra Madre Mountains to the Sierra de Sahuripa Mountains, and followed that range northward. We collected all the horses, mules, and cattle we wanted, and drove them northward through Sonora into Arizona. Mexicans saw us at many times and in many places, but they did not attack us at any time, nor did any troops attempt to follow us. When we arrived at our homes we gave presents to all, and the tribe feasted and danced. During this raid we had killed about fifty Mexicans.

Next year (1867) Mangus-Colorado led eight warriors on a raid into Mexico.[1] I went as a warrior, for I was always glad to fight the Mexicans. We rode south from near Tombstone, Arizona, into Sonora, Mexico. We attacked some cowboys, and after a fight with them, in which two of their number were killed, we drove all their

[1] Either Geronimo is in error here about the date of this raid (or Barrett, if it is he who worked out the chronology) or the leader of this raid was Mangus, son of Mangus-Colorado; the father had been cruelly tortured and then murdered by the whites in 1863. (FWT)

cattle northward. The second day we were driving the cattle, but had no scouts out. When we were not far from Arispe, Mexican troops rode upon us. They were well armed and well mounted, and when we first saw them they were not half a mile away from us. We left the cattle and rode as hard as we could toward the mountains, but they gained on us rapidly. Soon they opened fire, but were so far away from us that we were unable to reach them with our arrows; finally we reached some timber, and, leaving our ponies, fought from cover. Then the Mexicans halted, collected our ponies, and rode away across the plains toward Arispe, driving the cattle with them. We stood and watched them until they disappeared in the distance, and then took up our march for home.

We arrived home in five days with no victory to report, no spoils to divide, and not even the ponies which we had ridden into Mexico. This expedition was considered disgraceful.

The warriors who had been with Mangus-Colorado on this last expedition wanted to return to Mexico. They were not satisfied, besides they felt keenly the taunts of the other warriors. Mangus-Colorado would not lead them back, so I took command and we went on foot, directly toward Arispe in Sonora, and made our camp in the Sierra de Sahuripa Mountains. There were only six of us, but we raided several settlements (at night), captured many horses and mules, and loaded them with provisions, saddles and blankets. Then we turned to Arizona, traveling only at night. When we arrived at our camp we sent out scouts to prevent any surprise by Mexicans, assembled the tribe, feasted, danced, and divided the spoils. Mangus-Colorado would not receive any of this booty, but we did not care. No Mexican troops followed us to Arizona.

About a year after this (1868) Mexican troops rounded up all the horses and mules of the tribe not far from our settlement. No raids had been made into Mexico that year, and we were not expecting any attacks. We were all in camp, having just returned from hunting.

About two o'clock in the afternoon two Mexican scouts were seen near our settlement. We killed these scouts, but the troops got under way with the herd of our horses and mules before we saw them. It was useless to try to overtake them on foot, and our tribe had not a horse left. I took twenty warriors and trailed them. We found the stock at a cattle ranch in Sonora, not far from Nacozari, and attacked the cowboys who had them in charge. We killed two men and lost none. After the fight we drove off our own stock and all of theirs.

We were trailed by nine cowboys. I sent the stock on ahead and with three warriors stayed in the rear to intercept any attacking parties. One night when near the Arizona line we discovered these cowboys on our trail and watched them camp for the night and picket their horses. About midnight we stole into their camp and silently led away all their horses, leaving the cowboys asleep. Then we rode hard and overtook our companions, who always traveled at night instead of in the daytime. We turned these horses in with the herd and fell back to again intercept anyone who might trail us. What these nine cowboys did next morning I do not know, and I have never heard the Mexicans say anything about it; I know they did not follow us, for we were not molested. When we arrived in camp at home there was great rejoicing in the tribe. It was considered a good trick to get the Mexicans' horses and leave them asleep in the mountains.

It was a long time before we again went into Mexico or were disturbed by the Mexicans.

10

HEAVY FIGHTING

About 1873 we were again attacked by Mexican troops in our settlement, but we defeated them. Then we decided to make raids into Mexico. We moved our whole camp, packing all our belongings on mules and horses, went into Mexico and made camp in the mountains near Nacori. In moving our camp in this way we wanted no one to spy on us, and if we passed a Mexican's home we usually killed the inmates. However, if they offered to surrender and made no resistance or trouble in any way, we would take them prisoners. Frequently we would change our place of rendezvous; then we would take with us our prisoners if they were willing to go, but if they were unruly they might be killed. I remember one Mexican in the Sierra Madre Mountains who saw us moving and delayed us for some time. We took the trouble to get him, thinking the plunder of his house would pay us for the delay, but after we had killed him we found nothing in his house worth having. We ranged in these mountains for over a year, raiding the Mexican settlements for our supplies, but not having any general engagement with Mexican troops; then we returned to our homes in Arizona. After remaining in Arizona about a year we returned to Mexico, and went into hiding in the Sierra Madre Mountains. Our camp was near Nacori, and we had just organized bands of warriors for raiding the country, when our scouts discovered Mexican troops coming toward our camp to attack us.

BATTLE OF WHITE HILL

The chief of the Nedni Apaches, Whoa, was with me and commanded one division. The warriors were all marched toward the troops and met them at a place about five miles from our camp. We showed ourselves to the soldiers and they quickly rode to the top of a hill and dismounted, placing their horses on the outside for breastworks. It was a round hill, very steep and rocky, and there was no timber on its sides. There were two companies of Mexican cavalry, and we had about sixty warriors. We crept up the hill behind the rocks, and they kept up a constant fire, but I had cautioned our warriors not to expose themselves to the Mexicans.

I knew that the troopers would waste their ammunition. Soon we had killed all their horses, but the soldiers would lie behind these and shoot at us. While we had killed several Mexicans, we had not yet lost a man. However, it was impossible to get very close to them in this way, and I deemed it best to lead a charge against them.

We had been fighting ever since about one o'clock, and about the middle of the afternoon, seeing that we were making no further progress, I gave the sign for the advance. The war-whoop sounded and we leaped forward from every stone over the Mexicans' dead horses, fighting hand to hand. The attack was so sudden that the Mexicans, running first this way and then that, became so confused that in a few minutes we had killed them all. Then we scalped the slain, carried away our dead, and secured all the arms we needed. That night we moved our camp eastward through the Sierra Madre Mountains into Chihuahua. No troops molested us here and after about a year we returned to Arizona.

Almost every year we would live a part of the time in Old Mexico. There were at this time many settlements in Arizona; game was not plentiful, and besides we liked to go down into Old Mexico. Besides, the lands of the Nedni Apaches, our friends and kinsmen, extended far into Mexico. Their Chief, Whoa, was as a brother to me, and we spent much of our time in his territory.

About 1880 we were in camp in the mountains south of Casa Grande, when a company of Mexican troops attacked us. There were twenty-four Mexican soldiers and about forty Indians. The Mexicans surprised us in camp and fired on us, killing two Indians the first volley. I do not know how they were able to find our camp unless they had excellent scouts and our guards were careless, but there they were shooting at us before we knew they were near. We were in the timber, and I gave the order to go forward and fight at close range. We kept behind rocks and trees until we came within ten yards of their line, then we stood up and both sides shot until all the Mexicans were killed. We lost twelve warriors in this battle.

This place was called by the Indians "Sko-la-ta." When we had buried our dead and secured what supplies the Mexicans had, we went northeast. At a place near Nacori Mexican troops attacked us. At this place, called by the Indians "Nokode," there were about eighty warriors, Bedonkohe and Nedni Apaches. There were three companies of Mexican troops. They attacked us in an open field, and we scattered, firing as we ran. They followed us, but we dispersed, and soon were free from their pursuit; then we reassembled in the Sierra Madre Mountains. Here a council was held, and as Mexican troops were coming from many quarters, we disbanded.

In about four months we reassembled at Casa Grande to make a treaty of peace. The chiefs of the town of Casa Grande, and all of the men of Casa Grande, made a treaty with us. We shook hands and promised to be brothers. Then we began to trade, and the Mexicans gave us mescal. Soon nearly all the Indians were drunk. While they were drunk two companies of Mexican troops, from another town, attacked us, killed twenty Indians, and captured many more.[1] We fled in all directions.

[1] It is impossible to get Geronimo to understand that these troops served the general government instead of any particular town. He still thinks each town independent and each city a separate tribe. He cannot understand the relation of cities to the general government. (SMB)

11

GERONIMO'S MIGHTIEST BATTLE

AFTER the treachery and massacre of Casa Grande we did not reassemble for a long while, and when we did we returned to Arizona. We remained in Arizona for some time, living in San Carlos Reservation, at a place now called Geronimo. In 1883 we went into Mexico again. We remained in the mountain ranges of Mexico for about fourteen months, and during this time we had many skirmishes with Mexican troops. In 1884 we returned to Arizona to get other Apaches to come with us into Mexico.[1] The Mexicans were gathering troops in the mountains where we had been ranging, and their numbers were so much greater than ours that we could not

[1] These are references to a break from the reservation in 1881; the bulk of the hostiles returned in May 1883; Geronimo and his group returned to San Carlos in late February or early March 1884. (FWT)

122

hope to fight them successfully, and we were tired of being chased about from place to place.

In Arizona we had trouble with the United States soldiers and returned to Mexico.[2]

We had lost about fifteen warriors in Arizona, and had gained no recruits. With our reduced number we camped in the mountains north of Arispe. Mexican troops were seen by our scouts in several directions. The United States troops were coming down from the north. We were well armed with guns and supplied with ammunition, but we did not care to be surrounded by the troops of two governments, so we started to move our camp southward.

One night we made camp some distance from the mountains by a stream. There was not much water in the stream, but a deep channel was worn through the prairie, and small trees were beginning to grow here and there along the bank of this stream.

In those days we never camped without placing scouts, for we knew that we were liable to be attacked at any time. The next morning just at daybreak our scouts came in, aroused the camp, and notified us that Mexican troops were approaching. Within five minutes the Mexicans began firing on us. We took to the ditches made by the stream, and had the women and children busy digging these deeper. I gave strict orders

[2] An exceedingly oblique reference to the May 1885 break from the San Carlos Reservation—a break which was the result of an elaborate plan of Geronimo's and which I explain briefly in my introduction. (FWT)

to waste no ammunition and keep under cover. We killed many Mexicans that day and in turn lost heavily, for the fight lasted all day. Frequently troops would charge at one point, be repulsed, then rally and charge at another point.

About noon we began to hear them speaking my name with curses. In the afternoon the general came on the field and the fighting became more furious. I gave orders to my warriors to try to kill all the Mexican officers. About three o'clock the general called all the officers together at the right side of the field. The place where they assembled was not very far from the main stream, and a little ditch ran out close to where the officers stood. Cautiously I crawled out this ditch very close to where the council was being held. The general was an old warrior. The wind was blowing in my direction, so that I could hear all he said, and I understood most of it.[3] This is about what he told them: "Officers, yonder in those ditches is the red devil Geronimo and his hated band. This must be his last day. Ride on him from both sides of the ditches; kill men, women, and children; take no prisoners; dead Indians are what we want. Do not spare your own men; exterminate this band at any cost; I will post the wounded to shoot all deserters; go back to your companies and advance."

Just as the command to go forward was given I took deliberate aim at the general and he fell. In an instant the ground around me was riddled

[3] Geronimo has a fair knowledge of the Spanish language. (SMB)

with bullets; but I was untouched. The Apaches
had seen. From all along the ditches arose the
fierce war-cry of my people. The columns wa-
vered an instant and then swept on; they did not
retreat until our fire had destroyed the front
ranks.

After this their fighting was not so fierce, yet
they continued to rally and readvance until dark.
They also continued to speak my name with
threats and curses. That night before the firing
had ceased a dozen Indians had crawled out of
the ditches and set fire to the long prairie grass
behind the Mexican troops. During the confusion
that followed we escaped to the mountains.

This was the last battle that I ever fought with
Mexicans. United States troops were trailing us
continually from this time until the treatty was
made with General Miles in Skeleton Cañon.[4]

During my many wars with the Mexicans I
received eight wounds, as follows: shot in the
right leg above the knee, and still carry the bullet; shot through the left forearm; wounded in
the right leg below the knee with a saber; wounded on top of the head with the butt of a musket;
shot just below the outer corner of the left eye;
shot in left side, shot in the back. I have killed
many Mexicans; I do not know how many, for
frequently I did not count them. Some of them
were not worth counting.

It has been a long time since then, but still I
have no love for the Mexicans. With me they
were always treacherous and malicious. I am old
now and shall never go on the warpath again, but

if I were young, and followed the warpath, it would lead into Old Mexico.

*This was the final surrender of Geronimo and the Chiricahua, August 1886. (FWT)

PART III
The White Men

12

COMING OF THE
WHITE MEN

ABOUT the time of the massacre of "Kaskiyeh" (1858) we heard that some white men were measuring land to the south of us. In company with a number of other warriors I went to visit them. We could not understand them very well, for we had no interpreter, but we made a treaty with them by shaking hands and promising to be brothers. Then we made our camp near their camp, and they came to trade with us. We gave them buckskin, blankets, and ponies in exchange for shirts and provisions. We also brought them game, for which they gave us some money. We did not know the value of this money, but we kept it and later learned from the Navajo Indians that it was very valuable.

Every day they measured land with curious instruments and put down marks which we could not understand. They were good men, and we were sorry when they had gone on into the west. They were not soldiers. These were the first white men I ever saw.

About ten years later some more white men came. These were all warriors. They made their camp on the Gila River south of Hot Springs. At first they were friendly and we did not dislike them, but they were not as good as those who came first.

After about a year some trouble arose between them and the Indians, and I took the warpath as a warrior, not as a chief.[1] I had not been wronged, but some of my people had been, and I fought with my tribe; for the soldiers and not the Indians were at fault.

Not long after this some of the officers of the United States troops invited our leaders to hold a conference at Apache Pass (Fort Bowie). Just before noon the Indians were shown into a tent and told that they would be given something to eat. When in the tent they were attacked by soldiers. Our chief, Mangus-Colorado, and several other warriors, by cutting through the tent, escaped; but most of the warriors were killed or captured.[2] Among the Bedonkohe Apaches killed

[1] As a tribe they would fight under their tribal chief, Mangus-Colorado. If several tribes had been called out, the war chief, Geronimo, would have commanded. (SMB)

Fairly inaccurate: a war leader was a war leader whatever the circumstances. Geronimo's special function appears to have been that of an organizer and director of raids and wars. There *is* some confusion as to what such individuals did in times of peace; and it is this confusion which Barrett reflects here. (FWT)

[2] Regarding this attack, Mr. L. C. Hughes, editor of *The*

at this time were Sanza, Kladetahe, Niyokahe, and Gopi. After this treachery the Indians went back to the mountains and left the fort entirely alone. I do not think that the agent had anything to do with planning this, for he had always treated us well. I believe it was entirely planned by the soldiers.

From the very first the soldiers sent out to our western country, and the officers in charge of them, did not hesitate to wrong the Indians.[3] They never explained to the Government when an Indian was wronged, but always reported the misdeeds of the Indians. Much that was done by mean white men was reported at Washington as the deeds of my people.

The Indians always tried to live peaceably with the white soldiers and settlers. One day during the time that the soldiers were stationed at Apache Pass I made a treaty with the post. This

---

Star, Tucson, Arizona, to whom I was referred by General Miles, writes as follows:

"It appears that Cochise and his tribe had been on the warpath for some time and he with a number of subordinate chiefs was brought into the military camp at Bowie under the promise that a treaty of peace was to be held, when they were taken into a large tent where handcuffs were put upon them. Cochise, seeing this, cut his way through the tent and fled to the mountains; and in less than six hours had surrounded the camp with from three to five hundred warriors; but the soldiers refused to make fight." (SMB)

Barrett's note corrects Geronimo's mistake as to the principals involved in this incident, but it is doubtful if the Apache returned with three to five hundred warriors. (FWT)

[3] This sweeping statement is more general than we are willing to concede, yet it may be more nearly true than our own accounts. (SMB)

was done by shaking hands and promising to be brothers. Cochise and Mangus-Colorado did likewise. I do not know the name of the officer in command, but this was the first regiment that ever came to Apache Pass. This treaty was made about a year before we were attacked in a tent, as above related. In a few days after the attack at Apache Pass we organized in the mountains and returned to fight the soldiers. There were two tribes—the Bedonkohe and the Chokonen Apaches, both commanded by Cochise. After a few days' skirmishing we attacked a freight train that was coming in with supplies for the Fort. We killed some of the men and captured the others. These prisoners our chief offered to trade for the Indians whom the soldiers had captured at the massacre in the tent. This the officers refused, so we killed our prisoners, disbanded, and went into hiding in the mountains. Of those who took part in this affair I am the only one now living.

In a few days troops were sent out to search for us, but as we were disbanded, it was, of course, impossible for them to locate any hostile camp. During the time they were searching for us many of our warriors (who were thought by the soldiers to be peaceable Indians) talked to the officers and men, advising them where they might find the camp they sought, and while they searched we watched them from our hiding places and laughed at their failures.

After this trouble all of the Indians agreed not to be friendly with the white men any more. There was no general engagement, but a long struggle followed. Sometimes we attacked the white men—sometimes they attacked us. First a few Indians would be killed and then a few soldiers. I think the killing was about equal on each side. The number killed in these troubles did not amount to much, but this treachery on the part of the soldiers had angered the Indians and revived memories of other wrongs, so that we never again trusted the United States troops.[4]

---

[4] Geronimo here describes the Cochise wars extending throughout the 1860s and ending at the beginning of the '70s through the efforts of Thomas Jeffords and General O. O. Howard, both men who earned the trust of Cochise. (FWT)

13

GREATEST OF WRONGS

Perhaps the greatest wrong ever done to the Indians was the treatment received by our tribe from the United States troops about 1863. The chief of our tribe, Mangus-Colorado, went to make a treaty of peace for our people with the white settlement at Apache Tejo, New Mexico. It had been reported to us that the white men in this settlement were more friendly and more reliable than those in Arizona, that they would live up to their treaties and would not wrong the Indians.

Mangus-Colorado, with three other warriors, went to Apache Tejo and held a council with these citizens and soldiers. They told him that if he would come with his tribe and live near them, they would issue to him, from the Government, blankets, flour, provisions, beef, and all manner of supplies. Our chief promised to return to Apache Tejo within two weeks. When he came back to our settlement he assembled the whole

134

tribe in council. I did not believe that the people at Apache Tejo would do as they said and therefore I opposed the plan, but it was decided that with part of the tribe Mangus-Colorado should return to Apache Tejo and receive an issue of rations and supplies. If they were as represented, and if these white men would keep the treaty faithfully, the remainder of the tribe would join him and we would make our permanent home at Apache Tejo. I was to remain in charge of that portion of the tribe which stayed in Arizona. We gave almost all of our arms and ammunition to the party going to Apache Tejo, so that in case there should be treachery they would be prepared for any surprise. Mangus-Colorado and about half of our people went to New Mexico, happy that now they had found white men who would be kind to them, and with whom they could live in peace and plenty.

No word ever came to us from them. From other sources, however, we heard that they had been treacherously captured and slain. In this dilemma we did not know just exactly what to do, but fearing that the troops who had captured them would attack us, we retreated into the mountains near Apache Pass.

During the weeks that followed the departure of our people we had been in suspense, and failing to provide more supplies, had exhausted all of our store of provisions. This was another reason for moving camp. On this retreat, while passing through the mountains, we discovered four men with a herd of cattle. Two of the men were in front in a buggy and two were behind on horse-back. We killed all four, but did not scalp them; they were not warriors. We drove the cattle back into the mountains, made a camp, and began to kill the cattle and pack the meat.

Before we had finished this work we were surprised and attacked by United States troops, who killed in all seven Indians—one warrior, three women, and three children. The Government troops were mounted and so were we, but we were poorly armed, having given most of our weapons to the division of our tribe that had gone to Apache Tejo, so we fought mainly with spears, bows, and arrows. At first I had a spear, a bow, and a few arrows; but in a short time my spear and all my arrows were gone. Once I was surrounded, but by dodging from side to side of my horse as he ran I escaped. It was necessary during this fight for many of the warriors to leave their horses and escape on foot. But my horse was trained to come at call, and as soon as I reached a safe pace, if not too closely pursued, I would call him to me.[1] During this fight we scattered in all directions and two days later reassembled at our appointed place of rendezvous, about fifty miles from the scene of this battle.

About ten days later the same United States troops attacked our new camp at sunrise. The fight lasted all day, but our arrows and spears were all gone before ten o'clock, and for the re-

[1] Geronimo often calls his horses to him in Fort Sill Reservation. He gives only one shrill note and they run to him at full speed. (SMB)

mainder of the day we had only rocks and clubs with which to fight. We could do little damage with these weapons, and at night we moved our camp about four miles back into the mountains where it would be hard for the cavalry to follow us. The next day our scouts, who had been left behind to observe the movements of the soldiers, returned, saying that the troops had gone back toward San Carlos Reservation.

A few days after this we were again attacked by another company of United States troops. Just before this fight we had been joined by a band of Chokonen Indians under Cochise, who took command of both divisions. We were repulsed, and decided to disband.

After we had disbanded our tribe the Bedonkohe Apaches reassembled near their old camp vainly waiting for the return of Mangus-Colorado and our kinsmen. No tidings came save that they had all been treacherously slain.[2] Then

[2] Regarding the killing of Mangus-Colorado, L. C. Hughes of the Tucson, Ariz., *Star*, writes as follows: "It was early in the year '63, when General West and his troops were camped near Membras, that he sent Jack Swilling, a scout, to bring in Mangus, who had been on the warpath ever since the time of the incident with Cochise at Bowie. The old chief was always for peace, and gladly accepted the proffer; when he appeared at the camp General West ordered him put into the guard-house, in which there was only a small opening in the rear and but one small window. As the old chief entered he said: 'This is my end. I shall never again hunt over the mountains and through the valleys of my people.' He felt that he was to be assassinated. The guards were given orders to shoot him if he attempted to escape. He lay down and tried to sleep, but during the night, someone threw a large stone which struck him in the breast. He sprang up and in his delirium the guards thought

a council was held, and as it was believed that
Mangus-Colorado was dead, I was elected Tribal
Chief.

For a long time we had no trouble with anyone.
It was more than a year after I had been made
Tribal Chief that United States troops surprised
and attacked our camp. They killed seven children, five women, and four warriors, captured
all our supplies, blankets, horses, and clothing,
and destroyed our tepees. We had nothing left;
winter was beginning, and it was the coldest winter I ever knew. After the soldiers withdrew I
took three warriors and trailed them. Their trail
led back toward San Carlos.

---

he was attempting to escape and several of them shot him;
this was the end of Mangus.

"His head was severed from his body by a surgeon, and
the brain taken out and weighed. The head measured larger
than that of Daniel Webster, and the brain was of corre-
sponding weight. The skull was sent to Washington, and is
now on exhibition at the Smithsonian Institution." (SMB)

A reasonably accurate summary of this affair except that
the murder appears to have taken place in the open around
a camp fire and to have been preceded by extended torture
of the prisoner. (FWT)

14

REMOVALS

WHILE returning from trailing the Government troops we saw two men, a Mexican and a white man, and shot them off their horses. With these two horses we returned and moved our camp. My people were suffering much and it was deemed advisable to go where we could get more provisions. Game was scarce in our range then, and since I had been Tribal Chief I had not asked for rations from the Government, nor did I care to do so, but we did not wish to starve.

We had heard that Chief Victoria of the Chihenne (Oje Caliente) Apaches was holding a council with the white men near Hot Springs in New Mexico, and that he had plenty of provisions. We had always been on friendly terms with this tribe, and Victoria was especially kind to my people. With the help of the two horses we had captured, to carry our sick with us, we went to Hot Springs. We easily found Victoria and his band, and they gave us supplies for the winter. We stayed with them for about a year, and during this stay we had perfect peace. We had not the least trouble with Mexicans, white men, or Indians. When we had stayed as long as we should, and had again accumulated some supplies, we decided to leave Victoria's band. When I told him that we were going to leave he said that we should have a feast and dance before we separated.

The festivities were held about two miles above Hot Springs, and lasted for four days. There were about four hundred Indians at this celebration. I do not think we ever spent a more pleasant time than upon this occasion. No one ever treated our tribe more kindly than Victoria and his band. We are still proud to say that he and his people were our friends.

When I went to Apache Pass (Fort Bowie) I found General Howard in command, and made a treaty with him.[1] This treaty lasted until long after General Howard had left our country. He always kept his word with us and treated us as brothers. We never had so good a friend among the United States officers as General Howard. We could have lived forever at peace with him. If there is any pure, honest white man in the United States army, that man is General Howard.

[1] General O. O. Howard was not in command, but had been sent by President Grant, in 1872, to make peace with the Apache Indians. The general wrote me from Burlington, Vt., under date of June 12, 1906, that he remembered the treaty, and that he also remembered with much satisfaction subsequently meeting Geronimo. (SMB)

All the Indians respect him, and even to this day frequently talk of the happy times when General Howard was in command of our Post. After he went away he placed an agent at Apache Pass who issued to us from the Government clothing, rations, and supplies, as General Howard directed.[2] When beef was issued to the Indians I got twelve steers for my tribe, and Cochise got twelve steers for his tribe. Rations were issued about once a month, but if we ran out we only had to ask and we were supplied. Now, as prisoners of war in this Reservation, we do not get such good rations.[3]

Out on the prairie away from Apache Pass a man kept a store and saloon. Some time after General Howard went away a band of outlawed Indians killed this man, and took away many of the supplies from his store.[4] On the very next day after this some Indians at the Post were drunk on "tiswin," which they had made from corn. They fought among themselves and four of them were killed. There had been quarrels and feuds among them for some time, and after this trouble we deemed it impossible to keep the different bands together in peace. Therefore we separated,

[2] John P. Clum. For an account of his career as Apache agent see a book by that title written by his son, Woodworth Clum. (FWT)

[3] They do not receive full rations now, as they did then. (SMB)

[4] Apparently a reference to the killing of one Rogers and his cook Spence in April 1876, by a band of outlaw Apache under Skinya. The trouble between the Apache which resulted from this incident played a part in the decision of Geronimo and others to leave the reservation in June of the same year. (FWT)

each leader taking his own band. Some of them went to San Carlos and some to Old Mexico, but I took my tribe back to Hot Springs and rejoined Victoria's band.[5]

[5] This is Geronimo's laconic description of his break from the Fort Bowie Reservation in June 1876. In addition to the intratribal conflicts already alluded to, the Chiricahua were disturbed by the new orders from Washington that all the Apache were to be concentrated on the San Carlos Reservation. They had understood that the Fort Bowie home would be theirs forever, and both Victoria and Geronimo refused to go to San Carlos with the others. It should be noted that for the next year Geronimo and Victoria used Hot Springs as a raiding base. (FWT)

15

IN PRISON AND
ON THE WARPATH

Soon after we arrived in New Mexico two companies of scouts were sent from San Carlos. When
they came to Hot Springs they sent word for me
and Victoria to come to town. The messengers
did not say what they wanted with us, but as
they seemed friendly we thought they wanted a
council, and rode in to meet the officers. As soon
as we arrived in town soldiers met us, disarmed
us, and took us both to headquarters, where we
were tried by court-martial.[1] They asked us only
a few questions and then Victoria was released
and I was sentenced to the guardhouse. Scouts

[1] This very tense scene is glossed by Geronimo who was
ready to resist arrest to the death until he saw that the
odds in the form of Agent John P. Clum's Apache police
were against him. Sizing up the situation, he moved his hand
back from the hammer of his rifle and allowed that he was
ready for a smoke and a talk. See Woodworth Clum
(*Apache Agent*) for his father's firsthand recollection of
this affair. (FWT)

conducted me to the guardhouse and put me in chains. When I asked them why they did this they said it was because I had left Apache Pass.

I do not think that I ever belonged to those soldiers at Apache Pass, or that I should have asked them where I might go. Our bands could no longer live in peace together, and so we had quietly withdrawn, expecting to live with Victoria's band, where we thought we would not be molested. They also sentenced seven other Apaches to chains in the guardhouse.

I do not know why this was done, for these Indians had simply followed me from Apache Pass to Hot Springs. If it was wrong (and I do not think it was wrong) for us to go to Hot Springs, I alone was to blame. They asked the soldiers in charge why they were imprisoned and chained, but received no answer.

I was kept a prisoner for four months, during which time I was transferred to San Carlos. Then I think I had another trial, although I was not present. In fact I do not know that I had another trial, but I was told that I had, and at any rate I was released.

After this we had no more trouble with the soldiers, but I never felt at ease any longer at the Post. We were allowed to live above San Carlos at a place now called Geronimo. A man whom the Indians called "Nick Golee" was agent at this place. All went well here for a period of two years, but we were not satisfied.

In the summer of 1883 a rumor was current that the officers were again planning to imprison our leaders.[2] This rumor served to revive the memory of all our past wrongs—the massacre in the tent at Apache Pass, the fate of Mangus-Colorado, and my own unjust imprisonment, which might easily have been death to me. Just at this time we were told that the officers wanted us to come up the river above Geronimo to a fort (Fort Thomas) to hold a council with them. We did not believe that any good could come of this conference, or that there was any need of it; so we held a council ourselves, and fearing treachery, decided to leave the reservation. We thought it more manly to die on the warpath than to be killed in prison.

There were in all about 250 Indians, chiefly the Bedonkohe and Nedni Apaches, led by myself and Whoa. We went through Apache Pass and just west of there had a fight with the United States troops. In this battle we killed three soldiers and lost none.

We went on toward Old Mexico, but on the second day after this United States soldiers overtook us about three o'clock in the afternoon and we fought until dark. The ground where we were attacked was very rough, which was to our advantage, for the troops were compelled to dis-

[2] The chronology is faulty: the break described here took place at the end of September 1881. Geronimo's description of the motivating circumstances, however, sheds new and valuable light on actions assumed to represent simple lawlessness. The Chiricahua were alarmed by the presence of a large number of troops at San Carlos and by reports (perhaps deliberately circulated by civilians who stood to gain by the flight of the Indians) that they were to be tried for activities in past wars. (FWT)

mount in order to fight us. I do not know how many soldiers were killed, but we lost only one warrior and three children. We had plenty of guns and ammunition at this time. Many of the guns and much ammunition we had accumulated while living in the reservation, and the remainder we had obtained from the White Mountain Apáches when we left the reservation.

Troops did not follow us any longer, so we went south almost to Casa Grande and camped in the Sierra de Sahuaripa Mountains. We ranged in the mountains of Old Mexico for about a year, then returned to San Carlos, taking with us a herd of cattle and horses.[8]

Soon after we arrived at San Carlos the officer in charge, General Crook, took the horses and cattle away from us. I told him that these were not white men's cattle, but belonged to us, for we had taken them from the Mexicans during our wars. I also told him that we did not intend to kill these animals, but that we wished to keep them and raise stock on our range. He would not listen to me, but took the stock. I went up near Fort Apache and General Crook ordered officers, soldiers, and scouts to see that I was arrested; if I offered resistance they were instructed to kill me.

This information was brought to me by the Indians. When I learned of this proposed action I left for Old Mexico, and about four hundred

[8] A highly condensed account of the Apache campaign, 1881–May 1883. For further details see my introduction and for a firsthand account see Britton Davis, *The Truth About Geronimo*. (FWT)

Indians went with me.[4] They were the Bedon-kohe, Chokonen, and Nedni Apaches. At this time Whoa was dead, and Naiche was the only chief with me. We went south into Sonora and camped in the mountains. Troops followed us, but did not attack us until we were camped in the mountains west of Casa Grande. Here we were attacked by Government Indian scouts. One boy was killed and nearly all of our women and children were captured.[5]

After this battle we went south of Casa Grande and made camp, but within a few days this camp was attacked by Mexican soldiers. We skirmished with them all day, killing a few Mexicans but sustaining no loss ouselves.

That night we went east into the foothills of the Sierra Madre Mountains and made another camp. Mexican troops trailed us, and after a few days attacked our camp again. This time the Mexicans had a very large army, and we avoided a general engagement. It is senseless to fight when you cannot hope to win.

That night we held a council of war; our scouts had reported bands of United States and Mexican troops at many points in the mountains. We estimated that about two thousand soldiers were ranging these mountains seeking to capture us.

General Crook had come down into Mexico

[4] The break of May 17, 1885, which Geronimo engineered and for which he was almost executed by Naiche and Chihuahua when they discovered how he had tricked them. (FWT)

[5] Geronimo's whole family, excepting his eldest son, a warrior, were captured. (SMB)

with the United States troops. They were camped in the Sierra de Antunez Mountains. Scouts told me that General Crook wished to see me and I went to his camp. When I arrived General Crook said to me, "Why did you leave the reservation?" I said: "You told me that I might live in the reservation the same as white people lived. One year I raised a crop of corn, and gathered and stored it, and the next year I put in a crop of oats, and when the crop was almost ready to harvest, you told your soldiers to put me in prison, and if I resisted to kill me. If I had been let alone I would now have been in good circumstances, but instead of that you and the Mexicans are hunting me with soldiers." He said: "I never gave any such orders; the troops at Fort Apache, who spread this report, knew that it was untrue." Then I agreed to go back with him to San Carlos.[6]

It was hard for me to believe him at that time. Now I know that what he said was untrue, and I firmly believe that he did issue the orders for me to be put in prison, or to be killed in case I offered resistance.[7]

[6] Geronimo's account of the conference at Cañon de los Embudos, March 25, 27, 1886. The relevant sections of the stenographer's report of this conference are reproduced in Davis, *The Truth About Geronimo*. (FWT)

[7] Geronimo's exact words, for which the Editor disclaims any responsibility. (SMB)

16

THE FINAL STRUGGLE

WE started with all our tribe to go with General Crook back to the United States, but I feared treachery and decided to remain in Mexico. We were not under any guard at the time. The United States troops marched in front and the Indians followed, and when we became suspicious, we turned back. I do not know how far the United States army went after myself, and some warriors turned back before we were missed, and I do not care.[1]

I have suffered much from such unjust orders as those of General Crook. Such acts have caused much distress to my people. I think that General Crook's death was sent by the Almighty as a punishment for the many evil deeds he committed.

Soon General Miles was made commander of all the western posts, and troops trailed us con-

[1] The figures on the party which bolted into the hills vary. The two most frequently used are: twenty warriors, fourteen women, and two boys; or nineteen warriors, thirteen women, and six children. (FWT)

tinually.[2] They were led by Captain Lawton, who had good scouts. The Mexican soldiers also became more active and more numerous. We had skirmishes almost every day, and so we finally decided to break up into small bands. With six men and four women I made for the range of mountains near Hot Springs, New Mexico. We passed many cattle ranches, but had no trouble with the cowboys. We killed cattle to eat whenever we were in need of food, but we frequently suffered greatly for water. At one time we had no water for two days and nights and our horses almost died from thirst. We ranged in the mountains of New Mexico for some time, then thinking that perhaps the troops had left Mexico, we returned. On our return through Old Mexico we attacked every Mexican found, even if for no other reason than to kill. We believed they had asked the United States troops to come down to Mexico to fight us.

South of Casa Grande, near a place called by the Indians Gosoda, there was a road leading out from the town. There was much freighting carried on by the Mexicans over this road. Where the road ran through a mountain pass we stayed in hiding, and whenever Mexican freighters passed we killed them, took what supplies we wanted, and destroyed the remainder. We were reckless of our lives, because we felt that every man's hand was against us. If we returned to the

[2] As a result of Geronimo's escape General Crook resigned and was replaced by General Nelson A. Miles. (FWT)

reservation we would be put in prison and killed; if we stayed in Mexico they would continue to send soldiers to fight us; so we gave no quarter to anyone and asked no favors.

After some time we left Gosoda and soon were reunited with our tribe in the Sierra de Antunez Mountains.

Contrary to our expectations the United States soldiers had not left the mountains in Mexico, and were soon trailing us and skirmishing with us almost every day. Four or five times they surprised our camp. One time they surprised us about nine o'clock in the morning, and captured all our horses (nineteen in number) and secured our store of dried meats.[3] We also lost three Indians in this encounter. About the middle of the afternoon of the same day we attacked them from the rear as they were passing through a prairie —killed one soldier, but lost none ourselves. In this skirmish we recovered all our horses except three that belonged to me. The three horses that we did not recover were the best riding horses we had.

Soon after this we made a treaty with the Mexican troops. They told us that the United States troops were the real cause of these wars, and agreed not to fight any more with us provided we would return to the United States. This we agreed to do, and resumed our march, expecting to try to make a treaty with the United States

---

[3] Captain Lawton reports officially the same engagement (see page 187), but makes no mention of the recapture (by the Apache) of the horses. (SMB)

soldiers and return to Arizona. There seemed to
be no other course to pursue.

Soon after this scouts from Captain Lawton's
troops told us that he wished to make a treaty
with us; but I knew that General Miles was the
chief of the American troops, and I decided to
treat with him.[4]

We continued to move our camp northward,
and the American troops also moved northward,
keeping at no great distance from us, but not attacking us.

I sent my brother Porico (White Horse) with
Mr. George Wratton on to Fort Bowie to see
General Miles, and to tell him that we wished to
return to Arizona; but before these messengers
returned I met two Indian scouts—Kayitah, a
Chokonen Apache, and Marteen, a Nedni
Apache. They were serving as scouts for Captain
Lawton's troops. They told me that General
Miles had come and had sent them to ask me to

---

[4] Geronimo here describes his initial contact with Lieutenant Charles B. Gatewood, Lawton's advance scout, on
August 25, 1886, near Fronteras. The ragged band was
finished, militarily speaking, and Geronimo was suffering
from the effects of a three-day drunk. He sued for peace on
the terms originally offered by Crook in March (immediate reunion with families, a two-year imprisonment in the
East, and then return to the reservation), but was refused
and was apparently told that return to the reservation was
up to Washington. What happened thereafter is a matter
much in dispute as the material collected by Barrett in the
Appendix indicates. The clearest reconstruction I can make
from the available evidence is that Geronimo refused Gatewood's surrender proposition and determined to fight it out
to the last man; then he changed his mind on the condition
that the hostiles would be speedily reunited with their
families. This condition was apparently agreed to several
days later by General Miles, but it was not fulfilled. (FWT)

meet him. So I went to the camp of the United States troops to meet General Miles.[5]

When I arrived at their camp I went directly to General Miles and told him how I had been wronged, and that I wanted to return to the United States with my people, as we wished to see our families, who had been captured and taken away from us.

General Miles said to me: "The President of the United States has sent me to speak to you. He has heard of your trouble with the white men, and says that if you will agree to a few words of treaty we need have no more trouble. Geronimo, if you will agree to a few words of treaty all will be satisfactorily ararnged."

So General Miles told me how we could be brothers to each other. We raised our hands to heaven and said that the treaty was not to be broken. We took an oath not to do any wrong to each other or to scheme against each other.

Then he talked with me for a long time and told me what he would do for me in the future if I would agree to the treaty. I did not greatly believe General Miles, but because the President of the United States had sent me word I agreed to make the treaty, and to keep it. Then I asked General Miles what the treaty would be. General Miles said to me:[6] "I will take you under Government protection; I will build you a house; I will fence you much land; I will give you cattle, horses, mules, and farming implements. You will

[5] September 4, 1886. (FWT)
[6] For terms of treaty see Appendix. (SMB)

be furnished with men to work the farm, for you yourself will not have to work. In the fall I will send you blankets and clothing so that you will not suffer from cold in the winter time.

"There is plenty of timber, water, and grass in the land to which I will send you. You will live with your tribe and with your family. If you agree to this treaty you shall see your family within five days."

I said to General Miles: "All the officers that have been in charge of the Indians have talked that way, and it sounds like a story to me; I hardly believe you."

He said: "This time it is the truth."

I said: "General Miles, I do not know the laws of the white man, nor of this new country where you are to send me, and I might break their laws."

He said: "While I live you will not be arrested."

Then I agreed to make the treaty. (Since I have been a prisoner of war I have been arrested and placed in the guardhouse twice for drinking whisky.)

We stood between his troopers and my warriors. We placed a large stone on the blanket before us. Our treaty was made by this stone, and it was to last until the stone should crumble to dust; so we made the treaty, and bound each other with an oath.

I do not believe that I have ever violated that

treaty; but General Miles never fulfilled his promises.[7]

When we had made the treaty General Miles said to me: "My brother, you have in your mind how you are going to kill me, and other thoughts of war; I want you to put that out of your mind, and change your thoughts to peace."

Then I agreed and gave up my arms. I said: "I will quit the warpath and live at peace hereafter."

Then General Miles swept a spot of ground clear with his hand, and said: "Your past deeds shall be wiped out like this and you will start a new life."

[7] The criticisms of General Miles in the foregoing chapter are from Geronimo, not from the Editor. (SMB)

17

A PRISONER OF WAR

When I had given up to the Government they put me on the Southern Pacific Railroad and took me to San Antonio, Texas, and held me to be tried by their laws.[1]

In forty days they took me from there to Fort Pickens (Pensacola), Florida. Here they put me to sawing up large logs. There were several other Apache warriors with me, and all of us had to work every day. For nearly two years we were kept at hard labor in this place and we did not see our families until May, 1887. This treatment was in direct violation of our treaty made at Skeleton Cañon.

After this we were sent with our families to Vermont, Alabama, where we stayed five years and worked for the Government. We had no

[1] Geronimo narrowly escaped civilian trial at San Antonio for murder. The outcome of such a trial at that time and place would have been a foregone conclusion. His deportation to Florida was thus somewhat in the nature of an "escape." (FWT)

property, and I looked in vain for General Miles to send me to that land of which he had spoken; I longed in vain for the implements, house, and stock that General Miles had promised me.[2]

During this time one of my warriors, Fun, killed himself and his wife. Another one shot his wife and then shot himself. He fell dead, but the woman recovered and is still living.[3]

We were not healthy in this place, for the climate disagreed with us. So many of our people died that I consented to let one of my wives go to the Mescalero Agency in New Mexico to live. This separation is according to our custom equivalent to what the white people call divorce, and so she married again soon after she got to Mescalero. She also kept our two small children, which she had a right to do. The children, Lenna and Robbie, are still living at Mescalero, New Mexico. Lenna is married. I kept one wife, but she is dead now and I have only our daughter Eva with me. Since my separation from Lenna's mother I have never had more than one wife at a time. Since the death of Eva's mother I married another woman (December, 1905) but we could not live happily and separated. She went home to her people—that is an Apache divorce.[4]

[2] The Chiricahua were finally transported back to the West in August, 1894—not to their old homelands but to Fort Sill, Oklahoma. (FWT)

[3] According to Opler (*An Apache Life-Way*) these two incidents are one and the same. (FWT)

[4] These incidents and others indicate that Geronimo remained a difficult character to the end. His culturally induced (and perhaps temperamental) fierceness now had no legitimate outlet, and this evidently made him hard to live

Then, as now, Mr. George Wratton superintended the Indians. He has always had trouble with the Indians, because he has mistreated them.[5] One day an Indian, while drunk, stabbed Mr. Wratton with a little knife. The officer in charge took the part of Mr. Wratton and the Indian was sent to prison.

When we first came to Fort Sill, Captain Scott was in charge, and he had houses built for us by the Government. We were also given, from the Government, cattle, hogs, turkeys and chickens. The Indians did not do much good with the hogs, because they did not understand how to care for them, and not many Indians even at the present time keep hogs. We did better with the turkeys and chickens, but with these we did not have as good luck as white men do. With the cattle we have done very well, indeed, and we like

with. A semihumorous anecdote collected by Opler from a Chiricahua may help us to understand why Geronimo's marital life became so irregular:

"Geronimo was very absent-minded. He would be looking for his hat and he would have it on his head.

"One time when we were over to visit him, he was making a bow with a big knife. Pretty soon he began asking his wife where his knife was. All the time he had it in his hand, but we didn't let on. So there he was, scolding his wife and telling her to look for it for him. He was short and stout and pretty old, by then, so he wasn't active any more. That's why he wanted his wife to get it for him. But she wouldn't look. She said, 'You're old enough to look for your own knife.'

"Geronimo got pretty angry, 'Boys, you see how she is!' he said. 'I advise you not to get married.' Finally he saw the knife in his hand. 'Why, I'm nothing but a fool!' he said." (FWT)

[5] In Faulk's *The Geronimo Conspiracy* there is an episode which illustrates the racist way in which Wratton treated Indians in general and Geronimo in particular. (FWT)

to raise them. We have a few horses also, and have had no bad luck with them.

In the matter of selling our stock and grain there has been much misunderstanding.[6] The Indians understood that the cattle were to be sold and the money given to them, but instead part of the money is given to the Indians and part of it is placed in what the officers call the "Apache Fund." We have had five different officers in charge of the Indians here and they have all ruled very much alike—not consulting the Apaches or even explaining to them. It may be that the Government ordered the officers in charge to put this cattle money into an Apache fund, for once I complained and told Lieutenant Purington that I intended to report to the Government that he had taken some of my part of the cattle money and put it into the Apache Fund, he said he did not care if I did tell.[7]

Several years ago the issue of clothing ceased. This, too, may have been by the order of the Government, but the Apaches do not understand it.

If there is an Apache Fund, it should some day be turned over to the Indians, or at least they

[6] The Indians are not allowed to sell the cattle themselves. When cattle are ready for market they are sold by the officer in charge, part of the money paid to the Indians who owned them and part of it placed in a general (Apache) fund. The supplies, farming implements, etc., for the Apaches are paid for from this fund. (SMB)
[7] The criticism of Lieutenant Purington is from Geronimo. The Editor disclaims any responsibility for it, as in all cases where indivduals are criticized by the old warrior. (SMB)

should have an account of it, for it is their earnings.

When General Miles last visited Fort Sill I asked to be relieved from labor on account of my age. I also remembered what General Miles had promised me in the treaty and told him of it. He said I need not work any more except when I wished to, and since that time I have not been detailed to do any work. I have worked a great deal, however, since then, for, although I am old, I like to work and help my people as much as I am able.[8]

---

[8] Geronimo helps make hay and care for the cattle, but does not receive orders from the Superintendent of the Indians. (SMB)

PART IV
The Old
and the New

18

UNWRITTEN LAWS OF THE APACHES

TRIALS

WHEN an Indian has been wronged by a member of his tribe he may, if he does not wish to settle the difficulty personally, make complaint to the Chieftain. If he is unable to meet the offending parties in a personal encounter, and disdains to make complaint, anyone may in his stead inform the chief of this conduct, and then it becomes necessary to have an investigation or trial. Both the accused and the accuser are entitled to witnesses, and their witnesses are not interrupted in any way by questions, but simply say what they wish to say in regard to the matter. The witnesses are not placed under oath, because it is not believed that they will give false testimony in a matter relating to their own people.

The chief of the tribe presides during these trials, but if it is a serious offense he asks two or three leaders to sit with him. These simply determine whether or not the man is guilty. If he is not guilty the matter is ended, and the complaining party has forfeited his right to take personal vengeance, for if he wishes to take vengeance himself, he must object to the trial which would prevent it. If the accused is found guilty the injured party fixes the penalty, which is generally confirmed by the chief and his associates.

ADOPTION OF CHILDREN

If any children are left orphans by the usage of war or otherwise, that is, if both parents are dead, the chief of the tribe may adopt them or give them away as he desires. In the case of outlawed Indians, they may, if they wish, take their children with them, but if they leave the children with the tribe, the chief decides what will be done with them, but no disgrace attaches to the children.

"SALT LAKE"

We obtained our salt from a little lake in the Gila Mountains. This is a very small lake of clear, shallow water, and in the center a small mound arises above the surface of the water. The water is too salty to drink, and the bottom of the lake is covered with a brown crust. When this crust is broken cakes of salt adhere to it. These cakes of salt may be washed clear in the water of this lake, but if washed in other water will dissolve.

When visiting this lake our people were not allowed to even kill game or attack an enemy. All creatures were free to go and come without molestation.

PREPARATION OF A WARRIOR

To be admitted as a warrior a youth must have gone with the warriors of his tribe four separate times on the warpath.

On the first trip he will be given only very inferior food. With this he must be contented without murmuring. On none of the four trips is he allowed to select his food as the warriors do, but must eat such food as he is permitted to have.

On each of these expeditions he acts as servant, cares for the horses, cooks the food, and does whatever duties he should do without being told. He knows what things are to be done, and without waiting to be told is to do them. He is not allowed to speak to any warrior except in answer to questions or when told to speak.

During these four wars he is expected to learn the sacred names of everything used in war, for after the tribe enters upon the warpath no common names are used in referring to anything appertaining to war in any way. War is a solemn religious matter.

If, after four expeditions, all the warriors are satisfied that the youth has been industrious, has not spoken out of order, has been discreet in all things, has shown courage in battle, has borne all hardships uncomplainingly, and has exhibited no color of cowardice, or weakness of any kind, he may by vote of the council be admitted as a warrior; but if any warrior objects to him upon any account he will be subjected to further tests, and if he meets these courageously, his name may again be proposed. When he has proven beyond question that he can bear hardships without complaint, and that he is a stranger to fear, he is admitted to the council of the warriors in the lowest rank. After this there is no formal test for promotions, but by common consent he assumes a station on the battlefield, and if that position is maintained with honor, he is allowed to keep it, and may be asked, or may volunteer, to take a higher station, but no warrior would presume to take a higher station unless he had assurance from the leaders of the tribe that his conduct in the first position was worthy of commendation.

From this point upward the only election by the council in formal assembly is the election of the chief.

Old men are not allowed to lead in battle, but their advice is always respected. Old age means loss of physical power and is fatal to active leadership.

DANCES

All dances are considered religious ceremonies and are presided over by a chief and medicine men. They are of a social or military nature, but never without some sacred characteristic.

A DANCE OF THANKSGIVING

Every summer we would gather the fruit of the yucca, grind and pulverize it and mold it into cakes; then the tribe would be assembled to feast, to sing, and to give praises to Usen. Prayers of Thanksgiving were said by all. When the dance began the leaders bore these cakes and added words of praise occasionally to the usual tone sounds of the music.

THE WAR DANCE

After a council of the warriors had deliberated, and had prepared for the warpath, the dance would be started. In this dance there is the usual singing led by the warriors and accompanied with the beating of the "esadadene," but the dancing is more violent, and yells and war-whoops sometimes almost drown the music. Only warriors participated in this dance.

SCALP DANCE

After a war party has returned, a modification of the war dance is held. The warriors who have brought scalps from the battles exhibit them to the tribe, and when the dance begins these scalps, elevated on poles or spears, are carried around the camp fires while the dance is in progress. During this dance there is still some of the solemnity of the war dance. There are yells and war-whoops, frequently accompanied by discharge of firearms, but there is always more levity than would be permitted at a war dance. After the scalp dance is over the scalps are thrown away. No Apache would keep them, for they are considered defiling.[1]

A SOCIAL DANCE

In the early part of September, 1905, I announced among the Apaches that my daughter, Eva, having attained womanhood, should now put away childish things and assume her station as a young lady. At a dance of the tribe she would make her début, and then, or thereafter, it would be proper for a warrior to seek her hand in marriage. Accordingly, invitations were issued to all Apaches, and many Comanches and Kiowas, to assemble for a grand dance on the green by the south bank of Medicine Creek, near the village of Naiche, former chief of the Chokonen Apaches, on the first night of full moon in September. The festivities were to continue for two days and nights. Nothing was omitted in the preparation that would contribute to the enjoyment of the guests or the perfection of the observance of the religious rite.

To make ready for the dancing the grass on a large circular space was closely mowed.

The singing was led by Chief Naiche, and I, assisted by our medicine men, directed the dance.

First Eva advanced from among the women and danced once around the camp fire; then, ac-

---

[1] This is in keeping with the Chiricahua fear of all things connected with death.

Some Chiricahua claimed that they learned scalping from the Mexicans, and certainly the Mexicans did scalp Apache dead. It has also been claimed that the Apache scalped *only* Mexicans. (FWT)

companied by another young woman, she again advanced and both danced twice around the camp fire; then she and two other young ladies advanced and danced three times around the camp fire; the next time she and three other young ladies advanced and danced four times around the camp fire; this ceremony lasted about one hour. Next the medicine men entered, stripped to the waist, their bodies painted fantastically, and danced the sacred dances. They were followed by clown dancers who amused the audience greatly.

Then the members of the tribe joined hands and danced in a circle around the camp fire for a long time. All the friends of the tribe were asked to take part in this dance, and when it was ended many of the old people retired, and the "lovers' dance" began.

The warriors stood in the middle of the circle and the ladies, two-and-two, danced forward and designated some warrior to dance with them. The dancing was back and forth on a line from the center to the outer edge of the circle. The warrior faced the two ladies, and when they danced forward to the center he danced backward: then they danced backward to the outer edge and he followed facing them. This lasted two or three hours and then the music changed. Immediately the warriors assembled again in the center of the circle, and this time each lady selected a warrior as a partner. The manner of dancing was as before, only two instead of three danced together. During this dance, which continued until daylight, the warrior (if dancing with a maiden) could propose marriage, and if the maiden agreed, he would consult her father soon afterward and make a bargain for her.[2]

Upon all such occasions as this, when the dance is finished, each warrior gives a present to the lady who selected him for a partner and danced with him. If she is satisfied with the present he says good-by, if not, the matter is referred to someone in authority (medicine man or chief), who determines the question of what is a proper gift.

For a married lady the value of the present should be two or three dollars; for a maiden the present should have a value of not less than five dollars. Often, however, the maiden receives a very valuable present.

During the "lovers' dance" the medicine men mingle with the dancers to keep out evil spirits.

Perhaps I shall never again have cause to assemble our people to dance, but these social dances in the moonlight have been a large part of our enjoyment in the past, and I think they will not soon be discontinued, at least I hope not.

---

[2] Apache warriors do not go "courting" as our youths do. The associations in the villages afford ample opportunity for acquaintance, and the arranging for marriages is considered a business transaction, but the courtesy of consulting the maiden, although not essential, is considered very polite. (SMB)

19

AT THE WORLD'S FAIR

WHEN I was at first asked to attend the St. Louis World's Fair I did not wish to go. Later, when I was told that I would receive good attention and protection, and that the President of the United States said that it would be all right, I consented. I was kept by parties in charge of the Indian Department, who had obtained permission from the President. I stayed in this place for six months. I sold my photographs for twenty-five cents, and was allowed to keep ten cents of this for myself. I also wrote my name for ten, fifteen, or twenty-five cents, as the case might be, and kept all of that money. I often made as much as two dollars a day, and when I returned I had plenty of money —more than I had ever owned before.

Many people in St. Louis invited me to come to their homes, but my keeper always refused.

Every Sunday the President of the Fair sent for me to go to a wild west show. I took part in the roping contests before the audience. There were many other Indian tribes there, and strange people of whom I had never heard.

When people first came to the World's Fair they did nothing but parade up and down the streets. When they got tired of this they would visit the shows. There were many strange things in these shows. The Government sent guards with me when I went, and I was not allowed to go anywhere without them.

In one of the shows some strange men with red caps had some peculiar swords, and they seemed to want to fight.[1] Finally their manager told them they might fight each other. They tried to hit each other over the head with these swords, and I expected both to be wounded or perhaps killed, but neither one was harmed. They would be hard people to kill in a hand-to-hand fight.

In another show there was a strange-looking negro. The manager tied his hands fast, then tied him to a chair. He was securely tied, for I looked myself, and I did not think it was possible for him to get away. Then the manager told him to get loose.

He twisted in his chair for a moment, and then stood up; the ropes were still tied but he was free. I do not understand how this was done. It was certainly a miraculous power, because no man could have released himself by his own efforts.

In another place a man was on a platform speaking to the audience; they set a basket by

[1] Turks. (SMB)

the side of the platform and covered it with red calico; then a woman came and got into the basket, and a man covered the basket again with the calico; then the man who was speaking to the audience took a long sword and ran it through the basket, each way, and then down through the cloth cover. I heard the sword cut through the woman's body, and the manager himself said she was dead; but when the cloth was lifted from the basket she stepped out, smiled, and walked off the stage. I would like to know how she was so quickly healed, and why the wounds did not kill her.

I have never considered bears very intelligent, except in their wild habits, but I had never before seen a white bear. In one of the shows a man had a white bear that was as intelligent as a man. He would do whatever he was told—carry a log on his shoulder, just as a man would; then, when he was told, would put it down again. He did many other things, and seemed to know exactly what his keeper said to him. I am sure that no grizzly bear could be trained to do these things.

One time the guards took me into a little house that had four windows.[2] When we were seated the little house started to move along the ground. Then the guards called my attention to some curious things they had in their pockets. Finally they told me to look out, and when I did so I was scared, for our little house had gone high up in the air, and the people down in the Fair Grounds

[2] Ferris wheel. (SMB)

looked no larger than ants. The men laughed at me for being scared; then they gave me a glass to look through (I often had such glasses which I took from dead officers after battles in Mexico and elsewhere), and I could see rivers, lakes and mountains. But I had never been so high in the air, and I tried to look into the sky. There were no stars, and I could not look at the sun through this glass because the brightness hurt my eyes. Finally I put the glass down, and as they were all laughing at me, I, too, began to laugh. Then they said, "Get out!" and when I looked we were on the street again. After we were safe on the land I watched many of these little houses going up and coming down, but I cannot understand how they travel. They are very curious little houses.

One day we went into another show, and as soon as we were in it, it changed into night. It was real night, for I could feel the damp air; soon it began to thunder, and the lightnings flashed; it was real lightning, too, for it struck just above our heads. I dodged and wanted to run away, but I could not tell which way to go in order to get out. The guards motioned me to keep still, and so I stayed. In front of us were some strange little people who came out on the platform; then I looked up again and the clouds were all gone, and I could see stars shining. The little people on the platform did not seem in earnest about anything they did; so I only laughed at them. All the people around where we sat seemed to be laughing at me.

We went into another place and the manager took us into a little room that was made like a cage; then everything around us seemed to be moving; soon the air looked blue, then there were black clouds moving with the wind. Pretty soon it was clear outside; then we saw a few thin white clouds; then the clouds grew thicker, and it rained and hailed with thunder and lightning. Then the thunder retreated and a rainbow appeared in the distance; then it became dark, the moon rose and thousands of stars came out. Soon the sun came up, and we got out of the little room. This was a good show, but it was so strange and unnatural that I was glad to be on the streets again.

We went into one place where they made glassware. I had always thought that these things were made by hand, but they are not. The man had a curious little instrument, and whenever he would blow through this into a little blaze the glass would take any shape he wanted it to. I am not sure, but I think that if I had this kind of an instrument I could make whatever I wished. There seems to be a charm about it. But I suppose it is very difficult to get these little instruments, or people would have them. The people in this show were so anxious to buy the things the man made that they kept him so busy he could not sit down all day long. I bought many curious things in there and brought them home with me.

At the end of one of the streets some people were getting into a clumsy canoe, upon a kind of shelf, and sliding down into the water.[3] They seemed to enjoy it, but it looked too fierce for me. If one of these canoes had gone out of its path the people would have been sure to get hurt or killed.

There were some little brown people at the Fair that United States troops captured recently on some islands far away from here.[4]

They did not wear much clothing, and I think that they should not have been allowed to come to the Fair. But they themselves did not seem to know any better. They had some little brass plates, and they tried to play music with these, but I did not think it was music—it was only a rattle. However, they danced to this noise and seemed to think they were giving a fine show.

I do not know how true the report was, but I heard that the President sent them to the Fair so that they could learn some manners, and when they went home teach their people how to dress and how to behave.

I am glad I went to the Fair. I saw many interesting things and learned much of the white people. They are a very kind and peaceful people.[5] During all the time I was at the Fair no one tried to harm me in any way. Had this been among the Mexicans I am sure I should have been compelled to defend myself often.

[3] Shooting the Chute. (SMB)
[4] Igorrotes from the Philippines. (SMB)
[5] The reader should recall here that Geronimo was not without guile. His statements about white culture often have the appearance of cutting several ways. (FWT)

I wish all my people could have attended the Fair.[6]

---

[6] Geronimo was also taken to both the Omaha and the Buffalo Expositions, but during that period of his life he was sullen and took no interest in things. The St. Louis Exposition was held after he had adopted the Christian religion and had begun to try to understand our civilization. (SMB)

20

RELIGION

In our primitive worship only our relations to Usen and the members of our tribe were considered as appertaining to our religious responsibilities.[1] As to the future state, the teachings of our tribe were not specific, that is, we had no definite idea of our relations and surroundings in after life. We believed that there is a life after this one, but no one ever told me as to what part of man lived after death. I have seen many men die; I have seen many human bodies decayed, but I have never seen that part which is called the spirit; I do not know what it is; nor have I yet been able to understand that part of the Christian religion.

We held that the discharge of one's duty would

[1] The use of the word "primitive" here, a favorite pejorative term of whites to describe other cultures, makes one suspect that either translator Deklugie or Barrett substituted this word for something like "old" or "original." What follows is a faithful depiction of the relatively unorganized state of the Chiricahua cosmography. (FWT)

make his future life more pleasant, but whether that future life was worse than this life or better, we did not know, and no one was able to tell us. We hoped that in the future life family and tribal relations would be resumed. In a way we believed this, but we did not know it.

Once when living in San Carlos Reservation an Indian told me that while lying unconscious on the battlefield he had actually been dead, and had passed into the spirit land.

First he came to a mulberry tree growing out from a cave in the ground. Before this cave a guard was stationed, but when he approached without fear the guard let him pass. He descended into the cave, and a little way back the path widened and terminated in a perpendicular rock many hundreds of feet wide and equal in height. There was not much light, but by peering directly beneath him he discovered a pile of sand reaching from the depths below to within twenty feet of the top of the rock where he stood. Holding to a bush, he swung off from the edge of the rock and dropped onto the sand, sliding rapidly down its steep side into the darkness. He landed in a narrow passage running due westward through a cañon which gradually grew lighter and lighter until he could see as well as if it had been daylight; but there was no sun. Finally he came to a section of this passage that was wider for a short distance, and then closing abruptly continued in a narrow path; just where this section narrowed two huge serpents were coiled, and rearing their heads, hissed at him as he approached, but he showed no fear, and as soon as he came close to them they withdrew quietly and let him pass. At the next place, where the passage opened into a wider section, were two grizzly bears prepared to attack him, but when he approached and spoke to them they stood aside and he passed unharmed. He continued to follow the narrow passage, and the third time it widened and two mountain lions crouched in the way, but when he had approached them without fear and had spoken to them they also withdrew. He again entered the narrow passage. For some time he followed this, emerging into a fourth section beyond which he could see nothing: the further walls of this section were clashing together at regular intervals with tremendous sounds, but when he approached them they stood apart until he had passed. After this he seemed to be in a forest, and following the natural draws which led westward, soon came into a green valley where there were many Indians camped and plenty of game. He said that he saw and recognized many whom he had known in this life, and that he was sorry when he was brought back to consciousness.[2]

I told him if I knew this to be true I would not want to live another day, but by some means, if by my own hands, I would die in order to enjoy these pleasures. I myself have lain unconscious on the battlefield, and while in that condition

---

[2] This dream vision was a standard one among the Chiricahua and serves to remind us of the various and profound ways in which a culture influences the minds of its people. (FWT)

have had some strange thoughts or experiences; but they are very dim and I cannot recall them well enough to relate them. Many Indians believed this warrior, and I cannot say that he did not tell the truth. I wish I knew that what he said is beyond question true. But perhaps it is as well that we are not certain.

Since my life as a prisoner has begun I have heard the teachings of the white man's religion, and in many respects believe it to be better than the religion of my fathers. However, I have always prayed, and I believe that the Almighty has always protected me.

Believing that in a wise way it is good to go to church, and that associating with Christians would improve my character, I have adopted the Christian religion.[8] I believe that the church has helped me much during the short time I have been a member. I am not ashamed to be a Christian, and I am glad to know that the President of the United States is a Christian, for without the help of the Almighty I do not think he could rightly judge in ruling so many people. I have advised all of my people who are not Christians, to study that religion, because it seems to me the best religion in enabling one to live right.

[8] Geronimo joined the Dutch Reformed church and was baptized in the summer of 1903. He attends the services regularly at the Apache Mission, Ft. Sill Military Reservation. (SMB)

Later Geronimo was expelled from the church for incessant gambling. (FWT)

21

HOPES FOR THE FUTURE

I AM thankful that the President of the United States has given me permission to tell my story. I hope that he and those in authority under him will read my story and judge whether my people have been rightly treated.

There is a great question between the Apaches and the Government. For twenty years we have been held prisoners of war under a treaty which was made with General Miles, on the part of the United States Government, and myself as the representative of the Apaches. That treaty has not at all times been properly observed by the Government, although at the present time it is being more nearly fulfilled on their part than heretofore. In the treaty with General Miles we agreed to go to a place outside of Arizona and learn to live as the white people do. I think that my people are now capable of living in accordance with the laws of the United States, and we would, of course, like to have the liberty to return to that land which is ours by divine right. We are reduced in numbers, and having learned how to cultivate the soil would not require so much ground as was formerly necessary. We do not ask all of the land which the Almighty gave us in the beginning, but that we may have sufficient lands there to cultivate. What we do not need we are glad for the white men to cultivate.

We are now held on Comanche and Kiowa lands, which are not suited to our needs—these lands and this climate are suited to the Indians who originally inhabited this country, of course, but our people are decreasing in numbers here, and will continue to decrease unless they are allowed to return to their native land. Such a result is inevitable.

There is no climate or soil which, to my mind, is equal to that of Arizona. We could have plenty of good cultivating land, plenty of grass, plenty of timber and plenty of minerals in that land which the Almighty created for the Apaches. It is my land, my home, my fathers' land, to which I now ask to be allowed to return. I want to spend my last days there, and be buried among those mountains. If this could be I might die in peace, feeling that my people, placed in their native homes, would increase in numbers, rather than diminish as at present, and that our name would not become extinct.

I know that if my people were placed in that mountainous region lying around the headwaters of the Gila River they would live in peace and act according to the will of the President. They would be prosperous and happy in tilling the soil and learning the civilization of the white men, whom they now respect. Could I but see this accomplished, I think I could forget all the wrongs that I have ever received, and die a contented and happy old man. But we can do nothing in this matter ourselves—we must wait until those in authority choose to act. If this cannot be done during my lifetime—if I must die in bondage—I hope that the remnant of the Apache tribe may, when I am gone, be granted the one privilege which they request—to return to Arizona.

Appendix

THE SURRENDER OF GERONIMO

These materials related to the surrender of Geronimo and the Chiricahua originally followed Chapter XVI but more properly belong in an appendix. The reader interested in following further these negotiations should see Britton Davis, *The Truth About Geronimo*, Odie Faulk, *The Geronimo Campaign*, and Dan L. Thrapp, *The Conquest of Apacheria*. (FWT)

ON February 11, 1887, the Senate passed the following resolution:

"RESOLVED, That the Secretary of War be directed to communicate to the Senate all dispatches of General Miles referring to the surrender of Geronimo, and all instructions given to and correspondence with General Miles in reference to the same." These papers are published in the Senate Executive Documents, Second Session,

185

49th Congress, 1886–7, Volume II, Nos. 111 to
125. For an exhaustive account of the conditions
of Geronimo's surrender the reader is referred
to that document, but this chapter is given to
show briefly the terms of surrender, and corrobo-
rate, at least in part, the statements made by
Geronimo.

Upon assuming command of the Department
of Arizona, General Nelson A. Miles was
directed by the War Department to use most
vigorous operations for the destruction or capture of the hostile Apaches.

The following extracts are from instructions
issued April 20th, 1886, for the information and
guidance of troops serving in the southern portion of Arizona and New Mexico.

"The chief object of the troops will be to capture or destroy any band of hostile Apache Indians found in this section of the country, and to
this end the most vigorous and persistent efforts
will be required of all officers and soldiers until
the object is accomplished."

. . .

"A sufficient number of reliable Indians will be
used as auxiliaries to discover any signs of hostile
Indians, and as trailers."

. . .

"To avoid any advantage the Indians may have

by a relay of horses, where a troop or squadron commander is near the hostile Indians he will be justified in dismounting one-half of his command and selecting the lightest and best riders to make pursuit by the most vigorous forced marches until the strength of all the animals of his command shall have been exhausted."

•   •   •

The following telegrams show the efforts of the United States troops and the coöperation of Mexican troops under Governor Torres:

"Headquarters Division of the Pacific,
"Presidio of San Francisco, Cal.
"July 22, 1886.

"ADJUTANT GENERAL,
"Washington, D. C.:

"The following telegram just received from General Miles:

" 'Captain Lawton reports, through Colonel Royall, commanding at Fort Huachuca, that his camp surprised Geronimo's camp on Yongi River, about 130 miles south and east of Campas, Sonora, or nearly 300 miles south of Mexican boundary, capturing all the Indian property, including hundreds of pounds of dried meat and nineteen riding animals. This is the fifth time within three months in which the Indians have been surprised by the troops. While the results have not been decisive, yet it has given encouragement to the troops, and has reduced the numbers and strength of the Indians, and given them a feeling of insecurity even in the remote and almost inaccessible mountains of Old Mexico.'

"In absence of division commander.
"C. M. McKeever,
"Assistant Adjutant General."

"Headquarters Division of the Pacific,
"Presidio of San Francisco, Cal.
"August 19, 1886.

"Adjutant General,
"Washington, D. C.:
"Following received from General Miles, dated 18th:

" 'Dispatches to-day from Governor Torres, dated Hermosillo, Sonora, Mexico, from Colonels Forsyth and Beaumont, commanding Huachuca and Bowie districts, confirms the following: Geronimo with forty Indians is endeavoring to make terms of peace with Mexican authorities of Fronteraz district. One of our scouts, in returning to Fort Huachuca from Lawton's command, met him, Naiche, and thirteen other Indians on their way to Fronteraz; had a long conversation with them; they said they wanted to make peace, and looked worn and hungry. Geronimo carried his right arm in a sling, bandaged. The splendid work of the troops is evidently having good effect. Should hostiles not surrender to the Mexican authorities, Lawton's command is south of them, and Wilder, with G and M troops, Fourth

Cavalry, moved south to Fronteraz, and will be there by 20th. Lieutenant Lockett, with an effective command, will be in good position tomorrow, near Guadalupe Cañon, in Cajon Bonito Mountains. On the 11th I had a very satisfactory interview with Governor Torres. The Mexican officials are acting in concert with ours.'

"O. O. Howard,
"Major General."

General O. O. Howard telegraphed from Presidio, San Francisco, California, September 24, 1886, as follows:

". . . The 6th of September General Miles reports the hostile Apaches made overtures of surrender, through Lieutenant Gatewood, to Captain Lawton. They desired certain terms and sent two messengers to me (Miles). They were informed that they must surrender as prisoners of war to troops in the field. They promised to surrender to me in person, and for eleven days Captain Lawton's command moved north, Geronimo and Naiche moving parallel and frequently camping near it. . . . At Skeleton Cañon they halted, saying that they desired to see me (Miles) before surrendering."

After Miles's arrival he reports as follows:

"Geronimo came from his mountain camp amid the rocks and said he was willing to surrender. He was told that they could surrender as prisoners of war; that it was not the way of officers of the Army to kill their enemies who laid down their arms.

". . . Naiche was wild and suspicious and evidently feared treachery. He knew that the once noted leader, Mangus-Colorado, had, years ago, been foully murdered after he had surrendered, and the last hereditary chief of the hostile Apaches hesitated to place himself in the hands of the palefaces. . . ."

Continuing his report, General Howard says:

". . . I believed at first from official reports that the surrender was unconditional, except that the troops themselves would not kill the hostiles. Now, from General Miles's dispatches and from his annual report, forwarded on the 21st instant by mail, the conditions are plain: First, that the lives of all the Indians should be spared. Second, that they should be sent to Fort Marion, Florida, where their tribe, including their families, had already been ordered. . . ."

D. S. Stanley, Brigadier General, telegraphs from San Antonio, Texas, October 22, 1886, as follows:

". . . Geronimo and Naiche requested an interview with me when they first ascertained that they were to leave here, and in talking to them, I told them the exact disposition that was to be made of them. They regarded the separation of themselves from their families as a violation of the terms of their treaty of surrender, by which they had been guaranteed, in the most positive manner conceivable to their minds, that they should be united with their families at Fort Marion.

"There were present at the talk they had with me Major J. P. Wright, surgeon, United States Army; Captain J. G. Balance, acting Judge-advocate, United States Army; George Wratton, the interpreter; Naiche, and Geronimo.[1]

"The Indians were separated from their families at this place; the women, children, and the two scouts were placed in a separate car before they left.

"In an interview with me they stated the following incident, which they regard as an essential part of their treaty of surrender, and which took place at Skeleton Cañon before they had, as a band, made up their minds to surrender, and before any of them, except perhaps Geronimo, had given up their arms, and when they were still fully able to escape and defend themselves.

"General Miles said to them: 'You go with me to Fort Bowie and at a certain time you will go to see your relatives in Florida.' After they went to Fort Bowie he reassured them that they would see their relatives in Florida in four and a half or five days.

---

[1] Mr. George Wratton is now at Fort Sill, Oklahoma, acting as Superintendent of Apaches. He has been with the Apaches as interpreter and superintendent since their surrender. (SMB)

"While at Skeleton Cañon General Miles said to them: 'I have come to have a talk with you.' The conversation was interpreted from English into Spanish and from Spanish into Apache and *vice versa*. The interpreting from English into Spanish was done by a man by the name of Nelson. The interpreting from Spanish into Apache was done by José Maria Yaskes. José Maria Montoya was also present, but he did not do any of the interpreting.

"Dr. Wood, United States Army, and Lieutenant Clay, Tenth Infantry, were present.[2]

"General Miles drew a line on the ground and said, 'This represents the ocean,' and, putting a small rock beside the line, he said, 'This represents the place where Chihuahua is with his band.' He then picked up another stone and placed it a short distance from the first, and said, 'This represents you, Geronimo.' He then picked up a third stone and placed it a little distance from the others, and said, 'This represents the Indians at Camp Apache. The President wants to take you and put you with Chihuahua.' He then picked up the stone which represented Geronimo and his band and put it beside the one which represented Chihuahua at Fort Marion. After doing this he picked up the stone which represented the Indians at Camp Apache and placed it beside the other two stones which represented Geronimo and Chihuahua at Fort Marion, and said, 'That is what the President wants to do, get all of you together.'

[2] Dr. Leonard Wood, later Army Chief of Staff. (FWT)

"After their arrival at Fort Bowie General Miles said to them, 'From now on we want to begin a new life,' and holding up one of his hands with the palm open and horizontal he marked lines across it with the finger of the other hand and said, pointing to his open palm, 'This represents the past; it is all covered with hollows and ridges,' then, rubbing his other palm over it, he said, 'That represents the wiping out of the past, which will be considered smooth and forgotten.'

"The interpreter, Wratton, says that he was present and heard this conversation. The Indians say that Captain Thompson, Fourth Cavalry, was also present.

"Naiche said that Captain Thompson, who was the acting assistant adjutant general, Department of Arizona, told him at his house in Fort Bowie, 'Don't be afraid; no harm shall come to you. You will go to your friends all right.' He also told them 'that Fort Marion is not a very large place, and is not probably large enough for all, and that probably in six months or so you will be put in a larger place, where you can do better.' He told them the same thing when they took their departure in the cars from Fort Bowie.

"The idea that they had of the treaty of surrender given in this letter is forwarded at their desire, and, while not desiring to comment on the matter, I feel compelled to say that my knowledge of the Indian character, and the experience I have had with Indians of all kinds, and the corroborating circumstances and facts that have been brought to my notice in this particular case, convince me that the foregoing statement of Naiche and Geronimo is substantially correct."

Extract from the annual report (1886) of the Division of the Pacific, commanded by Major General O. O. Howard, U. S. Army.

> "Headquarters Division of the Pacific,
> "Presidio of San Francisco, Cal.
> "September 17, 1886.

"ADJUTANT GENERAL,
   "U. S. Army, Washington, D. C.:
   "GENERAL: I have the honor to submit the following report upon military operations and the condition of the Division of the Pacific for the information of the Lieutenant General, and to make some suggestions for his consideration:

* * *

   "On the 17th of May, 1885, a party of about fifty of the Chiricahua prisoners, headed by Geronimo, Naiche, and other chiefs, escaped from the White Mountain Reserve, in Arizona, and entered upon a career of murder and robbery unparalleled in the history of Indian raids.

   "Since then, and up to the time of my assuming command of this division, they had been pursued by troops with varying success.

   "After the assassination of Captain Crawford, on January 11, by the Mexicans, the hostiles asked for a 'talk', and finally had a conference on

March 25, 26, and 27, with General Crook, in the Cañon of Los Embudos, 25 miles south of San Bernardino, Mexico, on which latter date it was arranged that they should be conducted by Lieutenant Manus, with his battalion of scouts, to Fort Bowie, Ariz.

"The march commenced on the morning of March 28 and proceeded until the night of the 29th, when, becoming excited with fears of possible punishment, Geronimo and Naiche, with twenty men, fourteen women, and two boys, stampeded to the hills. Lieutenant Manus immediately pursued, but without success.

•   •   •

"Simultaneously with my taking command of the division Brigadier General Crook was relieved by Brigadier General Miles, who at once set out to complete the task commenced by his predecessor.

"Geronimo and his band were committing depredations, now in the United States and now in Mexico, and, being separated into small parties, easily eluded the troops, and carried on their work of murder and outrage.

"Early in May General Miles organized the hostile field of operations into districts, each with its command of troops, with specific instructions to guard the water holes, to cover the entire ground by scouting parties, and give the hostiles no rest.

"An effective command, under Captain Lawton, Fourth Cavalry, was organized for a long pursuit.

"On May 3 Captain Lebo, Tenth Cavalry, had a fight with Geronimo's band 12 miles southwest of Santa Cruz, in Mexico, with a loss of one soldier killed and one wounded. After this fight the Indians retreated southward followed by three troops of cavalry.

"On May 12 a serious fight of Mexican troops with the hostiles near Planchos, Mexico, resulted in a partial defeat of the Mexicans.

"On May 15 Captain Hatfield's command engaged Geronimo's band in the Corrona Mountains, suffering a loss of two killed and three wounded, and the loss of several horses and mules, the Indians losing several killed.

"On May 16 Lieutenant Brown, Fourth Cavalry, struck the hostiles near Buena Vista, Mexico, capturing several horses, rifles, and a quantity of ammunition.

"The usual series of outrages, with fatiguing chase by troops, continued until June 21, when the Mexicans engaged the hostiles about 40 miles southeast of Magdalena, Mexico, and after a stubborn fight repulsed them. . . .

·   ·   ·

"About the middle of August Geronimo and his band were so reduced and harassed by the tireless pursuit of the soldiers that they made offer of surrender to the Mexicans, but without coming to terms.

"Their locality thus being definitely known, disposition of the troops was rapidly made to act in conjunction with the Mexicans to intercept Geronimo and force his surrender.

"On August 25 Geronimo, when near Fronteraz, Mexico, recognizing that he was pretty well surrounded, and being out of ammunition and food, made overtures of capitulation, through Lieutenant Gatewood, Sixth Cavalry, to Captain Lawton. He desired certain terms, but was informed that a surrender as prisoner of war was all that would be accepted.

"The Indians then proceeded to the vicinity of Captain Lawton's command, near Skeleton Cañon, and sent word that they wished to see General Miles.

"On September 3 General Miles arrived at Lawton's camp, and on September 4 Naiche, the son of Cochise, and the hereditary chief of the Apaches, with Geronimo surrendered all the hostiles, with the understanding, it seems, that they should be sent out of Arizona.

"I am not informed of the exact nature of this surrender, at first deemed unconditional. . . .

. . .

"I am, sir, very respectfully, your obedient servant,

"O. O. HOWARD,
"Major General, United States Army"

STATEMENT OF W. T. MELTON,
ANADARKO, OKLAHOMA

From 1882 to 1887 I lived in southern Arizona, and was employed by the Sansimone Cattle Company.

In 1886 I was stationed in Skeleton Cañon, about 10 miles north of the boundary line between Arizona and Old Mexico, with J. D. Prewitt. It was our duty to ride the lines south of our range and keep the cattle of the Company from straying into Old Mexico.

One afternoon, when returning from our ride, we discovered an Indian trail leading toward our camp. We rode hurriedly out of the hills into a broad valley so that we could better discover any attacking parties of Apaches and if assailed have at least a fighting chance for our lives. We knew the Apaches under Geronimo were on the warpath, but they were far down in Old Mexico. However, our knowledge of the Indians led us to expect anything at any time—to always be ready for the worst.

When we reached the valley we struck a cavalry trail also headed for our camp. This was perplexing, for neither the Indians nor the soldiers seemed to have been riding fast, and both trails led toward our camp in Skeleton Cañon. This cañon was a natural route from Old Mexico to Arizona, and almost all bands of Indians, as well as detachments of United States troops, passed and repassed through this valley when going to Old Mexico or returning therefrom, but never before had two hostile bands passed through here at the same time and traveling in the same direction, except when one fled and the other pursued. What this could mean was a mystery to us. Could it be that the troops had not seen the Indians? Were the redskins trying to head the troops off and attack them in their camp? Were the troops hunting for those Indians? Could this be Lawton's command? Could that be Geronimo's band? No, it was impossible. Then who were these troops and what Indians were those?

Cautiously we rode to our camp, and nailed on the door of our cabin was this notice:

"BE CAREFUL, GERONIMO IS NEAR BY AND HAS NOT YET SURRENDERED.

"CAPT. LAWTON."

Then we understood.

A short distance above our cabin we found the camp of the troops and we had just finished talking with Captain Lawton, who advised us to remain in his camp rather than risk staying alone in our cabin, when up rode the chief, Geronimo. He was mounted on a blaze-faced, white-stockinged dun horse.

He came directly to Captain Lawton and through an interpreter asked who we were and what we wanted.

As soon as the explanation was given he nodded his approval and rode away.

Prewitt and I rode away with him. We were

well armed and well mounted and Geronimo was well mounted, but so far as we could see unarmed. I tried to talk with the chief (in English), but could not make him understand. Prewitt wanted to shoot him and said he could easily kill him the first shot, but I objected and succeeded in restraining him.[3] While we were arguing the chief rode silently between us, evidently feeling perfectly secure. All this time we had been riding in the direction of our horses that were grazing in the valley about a mile distant from our corral. When we came to a place about a half mile from Lawton's camp, where a spur of the mountain ran far out into the valley, Geronimo turned aside, saluted, said in fairly good Spanish, "*Adios, Señors,*" and began to ascend a mountain path. Later we learned that he was going directly toward his camp far up among the rocks. We rode on, drove our horses back to the corral and remained in our cabin all night, but were not molested by the Indians.

The next day we killed three beeves for the Indians, and they were paid for by Captain Lawton. On the second day two mounted Mexican scouts came to Lawton's camp. As soon as these Mexicans came in sight the Indians seized their arms and vanished, as it were, among the rocks.

Captain Lawton wrote an account of conditions and delivered it to the Mexicans, who with-

[3] Recently Mr. Melton told Geronimo of this conversation. The wily old chief laughed shyly and said, "What if Prewitt's pistol had been knocked out of his hand? Other men have tried to shoot me and at least some of them failed. But I'm glad he didn't try it." (SMB)

drew. After they had gone and their mission had been explained to Geronimo the Indians again returned to their camp and laid down their arms.

On the next day word reached camp that General Miles was approaching and the Indians again armed and disappeared among the rocks. (Many of the Apache squaws had field glasses and were stationed every day on prominent mountain peaks to keep a lookout.[4] No one could approach their camp or Lawton's camp without being discovered by these spies.)

Soon after General Miles joined Lawton's command Geronimo rode into camp unarmed, and dismounting approached General Miles, shook hands with him, and then stood proudly before the officers waiting for General Miles to begin conversation with him.

The interpreter said to Geronimo, "General Miles is your friend." Geronimo said, "I never saw him, but I have been in need of friends. Why has he not been with me?" When this answer was interpreted everybody laughed. After this there was no more formality and without delay the discussion of the treaty was begun. All I remember distinctly of the treaty is that Geronimo and his band were not to be killed, but they were to be taken to their families.

I remember this more distinctly, because the Indians were so much pleased with this particular one of the terms of the treaty.

[4] These field glasses were taken from soldiers and officers (Mexicans and Americans) whom the Apaches had killed. (SMB)

Geronimo, Naiche, and a few others went on ahead with General Miles, but the main band of Indians left under the escort of Lawton's troops.

The night before they left, a young squaw, daughter-in-law of Geronimo, gave birth to a child. The next morning the husband, Geronimo's son, carried the child, but the mother mounted her pony unaided and rode away unassisted—a prisoner of war under military escort.

On the afternoon of the day of the treaty Captain Lawton built a monument (about ten feet across and six feet high) of rough stones at the spot where the treaty was made. The next year some cowboys on a round-up camped at the place, and tore down the monument to see what was in it. All they found was a bottle containing a piece of paper upon which was written the names of the officers who were with Lawton.

After the Indians left we found one hundred and fifty dollars and twenty-five cents ($150.25) in Mexican money hidden in a rat's nest near where the Indians had camped.[5]

About ten o'clock on the morning after the Apaches and soldiers had gone away twenty Pimos Indians, accompanied by one white man, surrounded our camp and demanded to know of Geronimo's whereabouts. We told them of the treaty and they followed the trail on toward Fort Bowie.

That afternoon, thinking all danger from Apaches past, my partner, Prewitt, went to ride

[5] This was a stick nest built on top of the ground by a species of woods rat. (SMB)

the lines and I was left in camp alone. I was pumping water (by horse-power) at the well. when I saw three Indians rounding up our horses about half a mile away. They saw me but did not disturb me, nor did I interfere with them, but as soon as they had driven the bunch of horses northward over the hill out of sight I rode quickly off in another direction and drove another bunch of horses into the corral. The rest of the afternoon I stayed in camp, but saw no more Indians.

The next day we rode over the hill in the direction these Indians had gone and found that they had camped not three miles away. There were evidently several in the party and they had kept scouts concealed near the top of the hill to watch me, and to shoot me from ambush had I followed them. This we knew because we saw behind some rocks at the crest of the hill in the loose soil the imprints left by the bodies of three warriors where they had been lying down in concealment.

At their camp we found the head and hoofs of my favorite horse, "Digger," a fine little sorrel pony, and knew that he had served them for dinner. We followed their trail far into Old Mexico, but did not overtake them. We had been accustomed to say "it was Geronimo's band," whenever any depredation was committed, but this time we were not so positive.

·   ·   ·

We do not wish to express our own opinion, but to ask the reader whether, after having had the testimony of Apaches, soldiers, and civilians, who knew the conditions of surrender, and, after having examined carefully the testimony offered, it would be possible to conclude that Geronimo made an unconditional surrender?

Before passing from this subject it would be well also to consider whether our Government has treated these prisoners in strict accordance with the terms of the treaty made in Skeleton Cañon.

A SELECTED BIBLIOGRAPHY

Andrist, Ralph K. *The Long Death: The Last Days of the Plains Indians.* New York: Macmillan, 1964; Collier Books, 1969.

Clum, Woodworth. *Apache Agent: The Story of John P. Clum.* Boston: Houghton Mifflin, 1936.

Davis, Britton. *The Truth About Geronimo.* New Haven: Yale University Press, 1929.

Diaz, Bernal (del Castillo). *The Discovery and Conquest of Mexico, 1517–1521.* Edited by Genaro Garcia; translated by A. P. Maudslay, London: The Hakluyt Society, 1928; New York: The Noonday Press, 1956.

Farb, Peter. *Man's Rise in Civilization as Shown by the Indians of North America from Primeval Times to the Coming of the Industrial State.* New York: E. P. Dutton, 1968.

Faulk, Odie B. *The Geronimo Campaign.* New York: Oxford University Press, 1969.

Goodwin, Grenville. *The Social Organization of the Western Apache.* Chicago: University of Chicago Press, 1942.

Hyde, George. *Life of George Bent; Written From His Letters.* Edited by Savoie Lottinville. Norman, Oklahoma: University of Oklahoma Press. 1967.

Lockwood, Frank C. *The Apache Indians.* New York: Macmillan, 1938.

Opler, Morris E. *An Apache Life-Way.* Chicago: University of Chicago Press, 1941.

Pearce, Roy Harvey. *The Savages of America.* Baltimore: The Johns Hopkins University Press, 1965.

Schellie, Don. *Vast Domain of Blood; The Story of the Camp Grant Massacre.* Los Angeles: Westernlore, 1968.

Thrapp, Dan L. *The Conquest of Apacheria.* Norman, Oklahoma: University of Oklahoma Press, 1967.

ABOUT
FREDERICK W. TURNER

Frederick W. Turner, III, was born in Chicago in 1937 and was educated there and in Connecticut, Ohio and Pennsylvania. He has the two traditional degrees and a Ph.D. in Folklore from the University of Pennsylvania. He has taught in the English Departments of Haverford College, the University of Rhode Island and the University of Massachusetts and is the author of essays on Hawthorne, Melville, Malamud, Thomas Berger, D. H. Lawrence, and jazz music. Most of these reflect his childhood interests in mysteries, various forms of lying, baseball, and cowboys and Indians.

SEVEN ARROWS

Hyemeyohsts Storm

A unique and moving novel about the ways of the Plai People by a Northern Cheyenne.

Superbly illustrated—over 150 pictures of faces and plac birds and animals of the Plains—and eight-tone color pla of the 13 symbolic shields, designed by Hyemeyohsts Sto and painted by Karen Harris.

$4.95

To order by mail, send $4.95 per copy plus 25¢ per order for handling to Ballantine Cash Sales, P.O. Box 505, Westminster, Maryland 21157. Pease allow three weeks for delivery.